CIRCU...
IN SOUTH PEMBROKESHIRE

Hazards and Problems
Take Notice, Take Care

The author and the publishers stress that walkers should be aware of the dangers that may occur on all walks.

- check local weather forecast before walking; do not walk up into mist or low clouds
- use local OS maps side by side with walking guides
- wear walking boots and clothing
- do not take any unnecessary risks – conditions can change suddenly and can vary from season to season
- take special care when accompanied by children or dogs
- when walking on roads, ensure that you are conspicuous to traffic from either direction

Walks with History

Circular Walks
in
South Pembrokeshire

Paul Williams

First edition: 1997
Revised edition: 2009
© Text: Paul Williams

ISBN: 978-1-84524-073-8

Cover design: Alan Jones

First published in 1997 by Gwasg Carreg Gwalch

Revised edition published in 2009 by Llygad Gwalch,
Ysgubor Plas, Llwyndyrys, Pwllheli, Gwynedd LL53 6NG
☎ 01758 750432   📠 01758 750438
✆ books@carreg-gwalch.com
Web site: www.carreg-gwalch.com

**14 circular walks highlighting
Pembrokeshire's landscape beauty and heritage**

Easy directions for all walks and how to get there

Pubs and Cafes and Local Attractions

Information Centres and Youth Hostels

If you want to see and experience the best of Pembrokeshire then this is the book for you! 14 circular walks have been selected that highlight Pembrokeshire's outstanding landscape beauty and history.

Suitable for families and individuals all walks are easy to follow and clear directions are given, together with sketch maps to help you find the way. Simple directions on how to reach the start of each walk are listed, as are details of public transport.

Whether you choose to explore spectacular coastal scenery, hidden river valleys or magical Preseli uplands, or to follow in the footsteps of Neolithic settlers, Celtic saints and Norman adventurers, points of interest will explain what gives each area it's own brand of uniqueness. There is a quick reference guide to help you in your choice.

To further entice you there are pubs and cafés, wildlife parks, castles, churches and mills to visit. All Information Centres and Youth Hostels are listed, together with notes on camping and carvan sites. And if this is not enough then there are suggestions for further walks!

CONTENTS

The Walks

A. The North West and St Brides Bay (OS Maps 1:50 000 St David's and Haverfordwest 157; 1:25 000 Outdoor Leisure 36 South Pembrokeshire Walks 1-3, 35 North Pembrokeshire Walk 4)

B. The Daugleddau and South Pembrokeshire (OS Maps 1:50 000 Tenby 158; 1:25 000 Outdoor Leisure 36 South Pembrokeshire).

Features

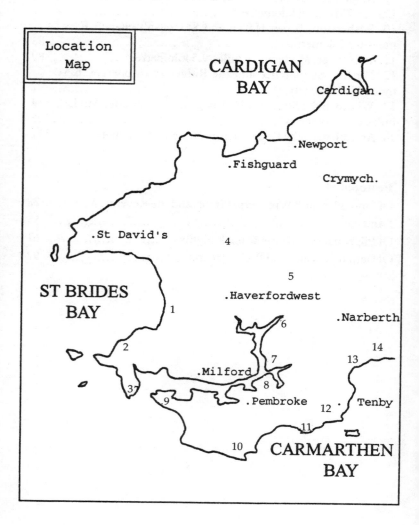

Location Map

CARDIGAN BAY

Cardigan .

.Newport

.Fishguard

Crymych.

.St David's

4

5

ST BRIDES BAY

.Haverfordwest

1

.Narberth

2

14

13

.Milford

7

8

3

9

.Pembroke

12 .

Tenby

11

10

CARMARTHEN BAY

8

INTRODUCTION

Out and About

One of the aims of this guide is simplicity. Walks are easy to follow, and clear directions are given. Another aim is variety. Walks have been selected that will highlight Pembrokeshire's outstanding landscape beauty and history. The exact location for the starting point of each walk is given, and how to get there. Relevant bus routes and numbers are included — though given that Pembrokeshire is a rural area services can be infrequent; eg perhaps only on Tuesdays! Nor do all buses operate on Sundays. Train services are also noted. Check with Information Centres for full details. The National Park occasionally operate a Coast Path bus service to the more popular coastal areas. There is adequate parking space at the start of each walk — precise details are given.

Walks vary in length from 2.5 miles/4 kilometres to 11 miles/17.5 kilometres — the latter a proper hill walk to whet the appetite! The routes utilise the long distance Pembrokeshire Coast Path, public footpaths, bridleways and the occasional permissive path. They are well maintained, and clearly signposted and waymarked — a yellow arrow or waymark indicating a public footpath, a blue one a bridleway. An acorn indicates the route is a long distance path, and is often confused with the, quite separate, National Trust's logo of an oak leaf! Many people are uncertain of how long a walk of e.g. 7 miles would take. As a rough guide an average walker would expect to cover 3 miles/4 kilometres an hour over level ground, on the ascent an hour for every 2000 feet/600 metres. Sketch maps for each walk are provided — all are based on the 1:25 000 series; however they can be no substitute for the definitive OS (Ordnance Survey) maps. The 1:50 000 maroon covered Landranger series (1.25 inches = 1 mile/2 centimetres = 1 kilometre) cover the county in 3 maps: Cardigan, St David's and Haverfordwest, and Tenby. Those preferring greater detail will wish to acquire the 1:25 000 series (2.5 inches = 1 mile/4 centimetres = 1 kilometre). The yellow covered Outdoor Leisure series cover the county in 2 maps: 35 North Pembrokeshire and 36

South Pembrokeshire. The green covered Pathfinder series are more numerous, covering as they do a much smaller area per map. The relevant maps for each walk are listed.

The grading system used is largely self-explanatory. Easy walks involve short walks over easy terrain, with little variation in contour. Moderate may have 1 or 2 short steep sections, with a little more variety in landscape, whilst strenuous will involve longer distances, with, perhaps, greater sections of ascent and descent, and over different types of terrain e.g. heather, woodland paths etc. Points of interest are included which are designed to give a quick snapshot of a particular area, what gives a place in landscape and historical terms it's own brand of uniqueness. Under facilities are listed alternative parking areas — as the walks are circular they may be joined at any convenient point, and details of parking at the most accessible points are listed. Also included are the nearest BT telephones, public toilets, cafés and pubs, Post Offices and shops, youth hostels, camping and caravan sites. Most small towns and many farms will offer B & B — check with Information Centres if you are interested. A separate list of all the youth hostels in the county is given under Other Information in the Appendix. Also listed under facilities are any additional places of interest in the neighbourhood e.g. wildlife parks, castles, mills.

Finally a word of warning. Footpaths get muddy, and cliffs can be dangerous. Take care! Ensure you have adequate clothing, and the proper footwear, i.e. boots or stout shoes, for each walk. Follow the Country Code!

Landscape and Culture

Pembrokeshire — the name is an anglicisation of the Welsh *Penfro*, or Land's End — juts out into the sea at the south west corner of Wales. Surrounded on three sides by the powerhouses of the Atlantic Ocean and the Irish Sea it's spectacular cliffs are studded with glittering coves and bays. One of the essential features of this landscape is it's many isolated peninsulas; another the extraordinary flatness of the land. Only the heather clad hills of the Preseli (home of the bluestones of Stonehenge), the great stone outcrops at Strumble Head, St David's and Treffgarne gorge, and the southern Ridgeway, rise above the uniformity. In the south, like a sword slash, the Milford Haven tears the plateau apart.

The county is renowned for it's magnificent coast and it's sandy shores, yet it has a magic and uniqueness which goes beyond these, for it is a microcosm of the major habitats to be found in Britain. The coastal waters are particularly rich in marine flora and fauna; the area around Skomer Island being designated Britain's second marine nature reserve after Lundy Island. The Dyfed coast plays host to some 5,000 grey seals; harbour porpoises and bottlenose dolphins are common sitings. The bird islands of Grassholm, Skomer and Skokholm are of international importance. Grassholm is the world's third largest gannetry, Skomer one of the world's top spots for the Manx shearwater. If razorbills and guillemots, fulmars, kittiwakes and puffins galore are main menu items then the islands are the places to visit! Fortunately the islands escaped the worst of the *Sea Empress* disaster, when in February 1996 70,000 tonnes of light crude oil were spilled into the sea from the stranded supertanker. However with oil reaching as far as Devon some thousands of oiled birds were the tragic result. Good mainland locations for birdwatchers are at Dinas Island, Strumble Head, and, in the south near Bosherston, at Stack Rocks and Stackpole Head.

Pembrokeshire's cliffs, at their highest in the north, are regal in spring and early summer. Magical yellows of gorse and bird's-foot trefoil mingle with the pinks of the thrift and the whites of sea campion. The succession of flowers continues, as if to order, from March to August. In the south are the main sand dune systems, extensive at Penally and Freshwater West, with smaller systems at Broad Haven South and Manorbier. Northern systems, some protected, are at Whitesand Bay, Newport and Poppit Sands. Sheltered behind shingle banks or sand bars are pockets of saltmarsh. Usually found at the mouths of estuaries they are hostile to all but the most salt tolerant plants. The Gann, at Pickleridge near Dale, is perhaps the most important, with others at Newport and the Teifi at Cardigan. Together with intertidal mudflats, formed by the accumulation of silt where fresh and salt waters meet, they are highly important feeding grounds for thousands of overwintering waders and wildfowl. The mudflats of Angle Bay, and the western and eastern arms of the Cleddau river, are particularly popular.

Freshwater habitats include the marshes found at the flood plains of rivers and streams. Good examples are at Penally, and at Pentood Marsh in Cilgerran Wildlife Centre. The largest area of open water in the National Park are the delightful lily ponds at Bosherston, a highly popular summer venue. Llysyfran Reservoir and Country Park, opened in the 1970s, attracts a number of winter waterfowl, as well as offering water sports and fishing. Remnants of the oak forest which once covered Pembrokeshire remain. Clinging to the sides of isolated valleys and hills, and along the steeper sections of river banks, they have unique beauty and atmosphere. The Gwaun valley in it's summer yellows and greens, or with the early morning mist rising from the water, is rightly famous, whilst hidden amongst the steep oak woods of the Cleddau are Norman river castles; whitewashed Benton opposite Lawrenny, or Carew, glimpsed through the trees bordering the Carew river. Less dramatic are the uniform stands of coniferous plantations which dot the uplands.

In the north of the county are the Preseli hills, extensive areas of lowland heath, acid grassland and moorland. They are predominantly heath, dominated by heather, with gorse in western areas giving way to bilberry in the east. Patches of wet heath or bogland, with sphagnum and cotton grass, break up the landscape. Smaller areas of low lying heath are at Strumble Head and St David's Head. Roadside verges, and traditional hedgebanks, whether of stone and/or turf, are ablaze with the colours of wild flowers in spring and early summer. The semi-natural specialised grassland of farms have less to offer in terms of wildlife, though many have areas of waste ground or a pond. In the south the limestone cliffs, and the plateau, with it's short springy turf and superb maritime flora, is one of the most impressive limestone areas in Britain.

Geologically Pembrokeshire is of spectacular interest. Not only does it offer magnificently exposed rock formations around it's coast, but the series of rocks on display range in an unbroken series from the very oldest Pre-Cambrian, from 3,000 million years ago, to the Carboniferous coal measures of 300 million years ago. The Pre-Cambrian rocks, formed before the appearance of any obvious fossilized life, occur in a small area extending from Whitesand Bay to Porth Llysgi. Later Lower Palaeozoic rocks, the Cambrian, Ordovician and Silurian systems which begin 570 million years ago, occur, like the Pre-Cambrian, in the north of the county. These igneous and sedimentary rocks were faulted and folded at the end of the Silurian period, some 400 million years ago, during the great Caledonian earth movements. As a result a WSW-ENE grain was imposed across the north of the county; one further result being the formation of St David's peninsula.

By contrast the rocks in southern Pembrokeshire are mainly Upper Palaeozoic. Devonian Old Red Sandstone covers most of the north side of Milford Haven, Dale and Angle peninsulas, and part of Caldey Island, while a superb limestone section runs from Linney Head to Stackpole Head, with further sections at Lydstep and Giltar Point at Penally. A significant coal measure runs across the county from Saundersfoot to St Brides Bay. After the depositions of the coal measures the land was again subject to massive earth movements, this time the Armorican orogeny of 290 million years ago. However now a WNW-ESE grain was imposed across the south of the county.

The present flatness of the land is due to constant wave erosion at a time when the sea covered the landscape, probably during the late Tertiary period some 17,000 million years ago. Only the more resistant igneous outcrops, like Carn Llidi and Garn Fawr, remained as islands above the sea. On at least 2 occasions Pemrokeshire lay under the Irish Sea glacier; the first occasion, some 120,000 years ago, covered the entire county, while the second, 20 to 17,000 years ago, affected only the north. Before the advent of this last ice sheet drove him south Palaeolithic man, Old Stone Age man, had made his appearance, living in caves on Caldey

Island and at Hoyle's Mouth near Penally. 150,000 years ago the climate became gradually warmer, and with the melting of the ice under the glacier deep and narrow gorges, originally formed with the initial retreat of the glacier, were further deepened as the meltwater scythed it's way to the sea. The Gwaun valley is the most impressive example of a meltwater channel in Britain.

With the final melting of the ice and the rise in sea levels 12,000 years ago the existing river valleys of Milford Haven and Solva were drowned by the incoming tides, assuming their present shape, and the forests were gradually submerged to remain exposed at coastal beaches, as at Whitesand Bay and Amroth, at low tides. At the time Mesolithic man appeared in the county, 10,000 years ago, Britain was still connected to Europe, however by 9,000 years ago Britain has assumed it's present status as an island. Mesolithic man continued to live, much as his ancestor Palaeolithic man had done, by hunting and fishing, with perhaps a little primitive farming, and some movement to open settlement in flimsy shelters. Finds of his flint tools have been made at Nab Head near St Brides Haven, Swanlake Bay near Manorbier, and on Caldey Island. Much of the marshy wooded lowlands where he hunted gradually fell under the encroaching sea — perhaps the tales of great floods, lost cities, and the fine towns of Cantref y Gwaelod (*the Low Hundred*) are folk memories of these drowned lands.

Around 3000 BC Mesolithic man was joined by Neolithic people arriving across the sea in simple craft, not unlike present day coracles. With them they brought the arts of agriculture — how to raise crops and herd animals. It was the Neolithic peoples who began the clearance of the native oak forest, living in flimsy houses, which, but for a single trace at Clegyr Boia near St David's, have disappeared. More enduring, comprising part of Europe's first architecture, are the great stone barrows, the cromlechau or collective burial chambers he left scattered throughout the county. Pentre Ifan near Nevern is one of the finest in Britain, with others, plentiful along the north coast and on the Preselis, rarer in the south. One theory has it that it was Neolithic man who transported the fabled bluestones from Carn Menyn in the Preseli to their present site at Stonehenge.

Circa 1800 BC marked the arrival of the Beaker people from the Low Countries and the Rhine — the name derives from the decorated pottery drinking vessels characteristic of the culture. They favoured individual burial beneath round barrows; Foel Drygarn in the Preselis is the finest example of this type. It was however the introduction of metal tools and weapons and the skills of metal working that transformed the old Mesolithic/Neolithic cultures into the Bronze Age. Stonehenge, in the wider context of Britain, was completed by the early Bronze Age, and is the crowning glory of this culture.

By 550 BC new settlers began to arrive from Gaul, workers in iron, whose traditional heartlands lay in central Europe. These were the Celts, ancestors of the Welsh and Irish. In complete contrast to the Neolithic and Bronze Ages, burial sites disappear from the landscape, to be replaced by easily identifiable hill forts and protected settlements. At St David's Head is one of the finest Iron Age sites, with stone hut circles, defensive walls and ditches and fields, all easily traceable. There are superb hill forts at Foel Drygarn, superimposed on the Bronze Age burial site, and at Carn Ingli; indeed any prominent feature or coastal promontory was seen as a possible settlement site by these warlike tribal people. It is probable that, before modern agriculture obliterated most of their traces, Iron Age settlements were as numerous in the landscape as present day farms. Castell Henllys, near Nevern, is a superb re-creation of an Iron Age settlement. The Roman occupation of 43-410 AD left Pembrokeshire and it's Celtic culture largely unmolested — there is a possible Roman villa site near Amroth, but other traces are very rare.

The 5th and 6th centuries saw a revitalisation of the Celtic culture, based on the new religion of Christianity and the lands around the Irish Sea. This was the Age of the Saints, when St David established his monastic settlement at St David's and St Patrick set out to convert Ireland. The movement was largely monastic, each monastery self-governing, with it's own rules and discipline. With it came a new mysticism and asceticism, something that seemed to suit the Celtic soul. Ascetics chose solitary places to reside, often living in clochàn — beehive shaped buildings made of local stone. There is at Pwll Deri, in Tal y Gaer farmyard, a building which may well have been a clochàn of this type. Pembrokeshire's coast is dotted with beaches and coves where the Celtic saints, the 'peregrini', landed and set sail for Ireland and beyond, and where the solitary could retire for meditation — St Govan's near Bosherston, with it's chapel in a cleft of rock, is the best known of these. Throughout the 9th and 11th centuries the coast was much troubled by Viking raiders, opportunists and adventurers, who gave their own names to many of the more prominent landmarks — Grassholm, Skokholm and Solva all have Norse connections. During this time St David's was burnt no less than 8 times. Truly trial by fire!

The Age of the Saints was also the heroic age of Britain, the age of Arthur, defender of civilisation after the Roman collapse to barbarism. The 11th and 12th century Welsh tales of the Mabinogion relate some of the earliest tales of Arthur in literature; Culwch and Olwen telling of Arthur and his knights' hunt of a magic boar across St David's peninsula, the Nyfer valley and the Preseli hills. However by the late 11th century a new master was in the land. At the time of the Norman invasion Pembrokeshire was part of the kingdom of Deheubarth, modern day Dyfed and the Gower. On the death of Deheubarth's ruler, Rhys ap Tewdwr, in 1093, the doors were open for Norman opportunists and adventurers. Moving from his base on the Severn, Roger, Earl of Shrewsbury, crossed into Pembrokeshire by way of Cardiganshire, his son establishing the Lordship of Pembroke.

The Normans never had sufficient power to retain the whole of Pembrokeshire, yet the failure of the Welsh to take Pembroke meant that the south of the county became detached from the north, with isolated Norman settlements in the north at Newport and Cilgerran. The new colony was nothing if not fragmented, with land parcelled out among incoming Norman adventurers, who established their forts and castles on the strategic high ground, most with access to river and sea. For a time a definable frontier stretched across the centre of the county from Roch Castle in the west to Amroth Castle on Carmarthen Bay — a frontier termed the Landsker by later historians. South Pembrokeshire formed part of the Marches of Wales, a region where taxes and law were the prerogatives of the Lords in the castle. The new colony was organised on the English pattern, the first such in Wales, and had, by at least 1138, independent 'palatine' status. This is the basis of Pembrokeshire's claim to be the premier county of Wales. Prior to the Norman arrival villages had been the largest settlements; with colonisation came the development of the Anglo-Norman towns, with Pembroke the first county town west of the Severn. The creation of 'Little England beyond Wales' was underway. The local population was absorbed into the growing Norman colony, supplemented by English, Irish and Flemish settlers. To the north, the Welsh maintained their way of life, and their own language — it was not until 1282 that, with the death of Llywelyn the Great, the independence of Wales, of which Deheubarth comprised a part, was finally ended during the Edwardian conquest. From then until the Tudor kings Wales was administered by Welsh and Anglo-Norman nobles, with the Marches as a buffer zone between Wales and England.

Along with Norman adventurism and militarism, often brutal, went great piety. William the Conqueror paid his respects at St David's in 1081. At no time was St David's ever garrisoned, though with growing Norman power an episcopal system was imposed, and, circa 1182, work began on a new cathedral. The Age of the Saints provided plenty of legends and holy sites for the growing number of pilgrims to St David's; hospitals were built for them by Norman bishops at Llawhaden and Whitewell at St David's, there were sisters' houses at Minwear on the eastern Cleddau, and possibly at Angle. Abbeys, priories and chapels were built, as at St Dogmaels, Haverfordwest and St Non's. The Knights Hospitallers of St John of Jerusalem had their Welsh headquarters at Slebech, on the opposite side of the river to Minwear, where they administered to the sick and recruited for the Crusades. Yet for all their piety there was a dark side to the Norman vision. The Celtic vision had been one of nature mysticism and humanity, the Normans introduced savage visions of heaven and hell.

The power of the Norman Lords and their independence was ended with the Act of Union of England and Wales in 1536. Pembrokeshire was made a county, with, for the first time, much the same boundaries as now, and the dissolution of the monasteries ended the power of the abbeys. Pilgrimages were now seen as idolaterous. A new faith was in the land, and all power was under the control of the king, Henry VIII. In the centuries that followed life came to be dominated by the demands of agriculture and trade. Those towns that had access to the sea grew into flourishing ports, and every small creek and cove seemed to have it's own sloop, often locally built. Out went wool, cattle and grain, and in came general merchandise, wine and spices, not to mention the often highly profitable smuggled cargo! The Civil War of the mid 17th century raised tensions and politics between neighbours — the Welsh mainly favoured the king, while the south were, usually, for Parliament — but if politics were uncertain and allegiances inconstant the underlying economy remained stable.

The 19th century had as profound effect on Pembrokeshire as had the arrival of the Normans. The coming of the railways in mid and late century heralded new communication and commercial advantages. Visitors began to arrive in increasing numbers at resort towns such as Tenby and Manorbier, already growing in importance during the late 18th century. 3 new towns were established on the shores around Milford Haven. Neyland, previously a small fishing village, was planned by Brunel as the terminus of his South Wales Railway, and as the terminus of Irish and transatlantic steamships — the latter functions transferring to Fishguard in the late 1900s. Milford Haven was laid out as a private initiative in 1793; among the earliest settlers a group of Quaker whalers from Nantucket, U.S.A. By 1900 to 1914 the town had risen to become one of the busiest fishing ports in the country. Across the water Pembroke Dock grew with the Admiralty dockyard established there in 1814 — for much of the century it was the world's most advanced shipyard, with revolutionary warships and 5 royal yachts to it's credit.

There were many local industrial concerns. Coal mining had always been of importance, production reaching it's peak during the late 18th and early 19th centuries at sites on St Brides Bay, at the confluence of the eastern and western Cleddau, and in the Saundersfoot and Kilgetty area. To exploit the latter's many pits the Saundersfoot Railway and Harbour Company was formed in 1829, and nearby, in Pleasant Valley, the Stepaside Ironworks flourished from 1849 to 1877. Whole villages were given over to quarrying, as at Cilgerran, and at Porthgain and Abereiddi where slates and bricks were also produced. Many of these concerns were comparatively shortlived, and had ceased operating by early or mid 20th century; Hook, on the western Cleddau, was the last colliery, closing in 1949, Porthgain's industrial age ended in 1931, and the Saundersfoot Railway and Harbour Company rail lines were raised by the 1940s. There were changes in agriculture too, cheap fertilizers raised yields and meant the end of the centuries old lime burning industry; cheap imported grain milled in larger town mills meant the end of local flour and feed producing mills; and cheap metals spelt the end of the local smithy. The revolution in land transport meant the end of the coastal trade, and local shipbuilding.

Politically the introduction of county councils in the late 1880s, with elected officials, replaced the centuries rule by the squierarchy, the local landowners who on a voluntary basis had occupied the leading positions in the county. The 19th century was also the hey-day of non conformism, active since the 17th century. Chapels, built out of subscriptions raised by local congregations, began to appear in ever increasing numbers in the towns and villages, particularly in the Welsh speaking areas. Indeed as public buildings the chapels are more truly the Welsh vernacular architecture than the great Norman castles. It was also the age of the restoration of the existing Norman and Celtic churches. Since the Reformation there had been little new church building, and existing churches had been either barely maintained or allowed to decay. Old ones were renovated, and new ones, with inventive variations on existing styles, were built, as at Capel Colman in the north east of the county near Boncath.

By the mid 20th century modernisation had transformed the county. 1960 saw the first oil port, Esso, established. The energy industry, agriculture and tourism, the public services and the small business sector are now the backbones of the local economy. Pembrokeshire was designated Britain's first coastal National Park in 1952, and the long distance Coast Path was opened in 1970. Pembrokeshire returned as a county in it's own right in April 1996, having been from 1974 part of the larger county of Dyfed (Pembrokeshire, Carmarthenshire, Cardiganshire) — the National Park was similarly made a separate authority.

The Country Code

Enjoy the countryside and respect it's life and work.

Guard against all risk of fire.

Fasten all gates.

Keep your dogs under close control.

Keep to the public paths across farmland.

Use gates and stiles to cross fences, hedges and walls.

Leave livestock, crops and machinery alone.

Take your litter home.

Help to keep all water clean.

Protect wildlife, plants and trees.

Take special care on country roads.

Make no unnecessary noise.

Welsh Place Names

Place names can be a fascinating study in their own right, indicating geographical features, patterns of former land ownership, forgotten buildings or former trades. However, the current place name may be far removed from the original name, particularly where there is an anglicised form of an old Welsh name e.g Pembroke is derived from Pen Fro, the Welsh for Land's End. Welsh place names are particularly expressive of geography, and can be highly poetic e.g. Pwll Deri, *pool of the oak trees*. Some of the more common names are listed below:

Aber — river mouth, estuary
Afon — river
Allt — wood, hill, slope
Bach/Fach — little
Bedd — grave
Bryn — hill
Bwlch — pass
Caer(au) — fort(s)
Canol — middle, centre
Capel — chapel
Carn — cairn
Carreg, pl. cerrig — rock, stone
Castell — castle
Cemais — river bend
Cleddau — sword
Coch — red
Coed — wood
Coetan — quoit
Cors — bog, marsh
Craig — rock, cliff
Crib — ridge
Croes — cross
Cromlech(au) — burial mound(s)
Cwm — valley
Cwrw — beer

Cyhoeddus — public
Dan — under
Dau — two
Deri — oak
Dinas — hill fort
Dôl — meadow
Du, Ddu — black
Dŵr — water
Dyffryn — valley
Efail — smithy
Eglwys — church
Ffordd — road
Ffos — ditch, dyke
Ffynnon — spring, well
Gain — fair, fine, elegant
Garn — cairn
Gelli — grove
Glan — river bank
Gors — bog, marsh
Gwastad — level, flat
Gwaun — moor, meadow
Gwyn — white
Gwynt — wind
Hafod — summer dwelling
Hen — old

Hendre — winter dwelling
Isaf — lower
Llan — church
Llannerch — clearing, glade
Llyn — lake
Llwybr — path/track
Llwyd — grey
Maen — rock/stone
Maes — field
Mawr/Fawr — great, big
Melin — mill
Melyn — yellow
Moel/Foel — bare topped hill
Morfa — marsh
Mynach — monk
Mynachlog — monastery
Mynydd — mountain
Nant — brook, stream
Newydd — new
Nos — night
Ogof — cave

Parc — field, park
Pen — head, top
Penrhyn — promontory, headland
Pentre — village
Plas — hall
Pont — bridge
Porth — harbour
Pwll — pool
Rhiw — hill
Rhos — moorland
Rhyd — ford
Sych — dry
Tafarn — inn
Traeth — beach
Tref — town, hamlet
Tŷ — house
Uchaf — upper
Y, Yr — the
Yn — in
Ynys — island
Ysgol — school

A few notes on pronunciation may help:

c — k (hard)
ch — as in lo*ch*
dd — th as in *th*at
f — v
ff — f
g — g (hard)
ll — pronounce l, keep tongue in position at roof of mouth, and hiss!
the — th as in *th*ink

There are 7 vowels, a,e,i,o,u,w and y. Pronunciation may be long or short.

w may be as in pool, or pull e.g. *cwm* (coom) — valley
y may be as in fun, or pin e.g. *y*, *yr* (u, ur) — the, *dyffryn* (dufrin) — valley

Many Welsh words change their pronunciation and spelling under certain circumstances e.g. the initial consonant of many words may soften: b to f, c to g, m to f, p to b etc. Common examples of mutations are *bach* (little) to *fach*; *mawr* (big) to *fawr*, *porth* (harbour) to *borth*. Such mutations can make tracing words through a dictionary a little problematic for the uninitiated!

Quick Reference Guide:

For those who have a particular interest in one type of walk e.g. woodland walks, or in a particular subject e.g. Neolithic burial chambers, or Bronze Age standing stones and hill forts, the following quick reference guide is given. The list is not exhaustive, and only the principal types, or sites, are indicated.

Coastal Walks: 1-3,9-11,13,14.
Beaches: good sandy beaches suitable for swimming feature on
    Walks: 1-3,9-14.
Hill Walks: 4.
Riverside Walks: 5-8.
Woodland Walks: 1,5-8,13,14.

Stone Age i.e. Palaeolithic, Mesolithic and Neolithic sites:
    2,10-12.
Bronze and Iron Age sites: 4,12.
Age of the Saints: 1,10,12.
Normans: 5,6,8,9,11. Castles feature on Walk 5 (Llawhaden), and
    11 (Manorbier).
Industrial Heritage sites e.g. mills, mining, shipbuilding,
    quarries: 4,6,7,13,14.

Information Centres ★ (Open all year)

Tourist Information Centres:

Cardigan, Theatre Mwldan ★ 01239 613230
Fishguard, 4 Hamilton Street ★ 01348 873484
Fishguard Harbour ★ 01348 872037
Haverfordwest, The Old Bridge ★ 01437 763110
Milford Haven, 94 Charles Street 01646 690866
Narberth, Town Hall, Market Street ★ 01834 860061
Pembroke, Commons Road ★ 01646 622388
Pembroke Dock, Guntower, Front Street 01646 622246
St David's, City Hall, High Street 01437 720392
Saundersfoot, Harbour Car Park 01834 813672
Tenby, The Croft ★ 01834 842404

Weather Services

Weathercall: Pembrokeshire,
Carmarthenshire, Cardiganshire
and Powys 0891 500414
Marinecall: Wales 0891 505360
Pembrokeshire County Council
(seasonal) 01834 812516

More Walks

The Daugleddau Trail
A circular trail around the Daugleddau estuary above the Cleddau Bridge, via Haverfordwest, Blackpool Mill, Lawrenny, Carew and Llangwm.

Ffos y Mynach (The Monk's Dyke)
A 5 mile/8 kilometre walk across St David's peninsula, from Pen Beri in the north to Ogof y Ffos, near Caer Bwdy Bay, in the south. Leaflet available from Information Centres. Can be combined with the Coast Path to make a circular walk of nearly 20 miles/30 kilometres.

The Golden Road
A long distance route from Crymych across the Preseli hills to Foel

Eryri. Can be easily extended by following Gwaun valley footpaths down to Fishguard.

The Knights' Way

A 9 mile/14.5 kilometre path from Blackpool Mill on the eastern Cleddau to Amroth on Carmarthen Bay, via Templeton and Colby Lodge. Leaflet available from Information Centres. The walk is highlighted on the 1:25 000 Outdoor Leisure map for South Pembrokeshire. Provides a link between the Daugleddau Trail and the Coast Path.

The Landsker Borderlands Trail

A 60 mile/95 kilometre circular walk taking in south eastern Pembrokeshire and western Carmarthenshire, with Narberth at it's centre. Leaflet/booklet available from Information Centres. The walk is highlighted on the 1:25 000 Outdoor Leisure map for South Pembrokeshire.

Llysyfran Reservoir and Country Park

There is a fine 7.5 miles/12 kilometres walk around the reservoir. The reservoir is particularly popular with the fishing fraternity — notable especially for it's trout.

The Pembrokeshire Coast Path

One of the national long distance trails. Starts in St Dogmaels near Cardigan, ending at Amroth on the Carmarthenshire border. 186 miles/300 kilometres officially, but in reality nearer 200 miles/320 kilometres.

Information Centres   * (Open all year)

Pembrokeshire Coast National Park Information Centres:

Broad Haven, National Park Car Park 01437 781412
Haverfordwest, 40 High Street 01437 760136
Newport, Banks Cottages, Long Street 01239 820912
Pembroke, 8a Castle Terrace 01646 682148
Saundersfoot, Harbour Car Park 01834 811411
St David's, City Hall, High Street 01437 720392
Tenby, The Croft * 01834 842404

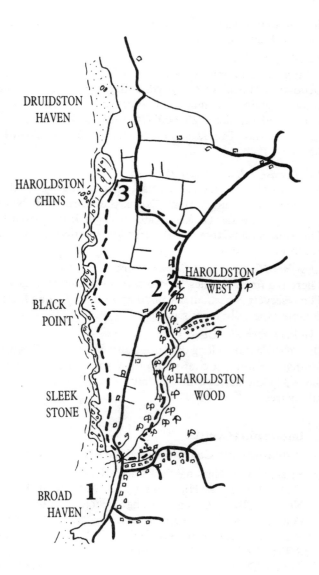

DRUIDSTON
HAVEN

HAROLDSTON
CHINS

3

BLACK
POINT

HAROLDSTON
WEST

2

HAROLDSTON
WOOD

SLEEK
STONE

BROAD
HAVEN

1

Broad Haven - Haroldston Wood
- Haroldston West - Haroldston Chins
- Broad Haven

OS Maps:	1:50 000 St David's and Haverfordwest 157; 1:25 000 Outdoor Leisure 36 South Pembrokeshire/ Haverfordwest (Hwlffordd) 1079 (SM 89/91).
Start:	Broad Haven National Park Information Centre, situated in the National Park car park.
Access:	Broad Haven is situated on the coast 5 miles/8 kilometres from Haverfordwest on the B4341. Can also be reached on the coastal roads from Newgale and Nolton Haven, and St Brides and Dale. Bus 311 from Haverfordwest stops at Broad Haven en route to Little Haven.
Parking:	National Park car park in Broad Haven, seasonal charge — or free parking in Broad Haven village, if you are lucky!
Grade:	Easy — woodland and coastal paths — some road walking.

Points of Interest:

1. Broad Haven has been a popular place since the beginning of the 19th century. Good for bathing and water sports it's expanse of golden sand links with Little Haven's at low tide, making it one of the finest beaches in St Brides Bay. Lion Rock, guarding Broad Haven's north end, protects Den's Door, 2 natural arches set into the superb sea stack standing out from the Sleek Stone and the rock folds of the sheer cliff behind. Access at low tide only! Haroldston Wood, sheltering the stream running down to Broad Haven's northern shore, is of recent origin, having been planted in the 19th

century for hunting. Plenty of oak and ash, with sallow, hazel, thorn and gorse, plus nesting boxes for the local residents!

2. Haroldston, Harold's enclosure or village, takes it's name from Harold de Harian Idystole, a Norman landowner who is known to have claimed lordship here in the early 14th century. The church itself, now totally altered, would have been founded much earlier, probably by St Aidan, or a follower of his, and who was an Irish pupil of St David in the 6th century — there is another church reputedly founded by St Aidan at Llawhaden, near Narberth. Rather confusingly St Aidan is also known as Edan, Mogue, Maidoc and Madoc; apparently the Irish root of his name means little fire (aid-an), or my little fire (mo-aid-oc). Easy when you know how! He was later to become the first Bishop of Ferns, in Ireland.

The site of the church would have been chosen with care. First there was the Celtic love of asceticism and solitude. Chapels and cells were founded in isolated places away from the main centres of habitation; siting them near springs and wells guaranteed water for survival and baptism — there are springs still bubbling to the east of the church. Again the site was on the old Neolithic and Bronze Age trackway leading from Monks Haven, near Dale, to Whitesand Bay. This 'Welsh Way' would have given safer passage to St David's new settlement than the more treacherous sea routes across St Brides Bay. The church would also have acted as a lookout point over the surrounding countryside. Prominent hilltop and coastal churches would also have acted as beacons for sea travellers. Nearby Walton West church had a tower added to it in the 14th century. The present church here was substantially rebuilt in the late 19th century.

Of Smugglers and Wreckers, Pirates, and the Revenue Men

The history of smuggling in Pembrokeshire has been one of official local condemnation, yet unofficial sanction. From Tudor times to the 19th century smuggling ventures were commonplace, and took place in hidden creeks and coves, often with the connivance of magistrates and Customs

28

officials. Cargoes of tea, tobacco, wine, spirits, salt, spices and coal were stock in trade. Ship's masters, operating legal businesses out of local ports, used to add a little extra cargo by way of added interest and income. Professional smugglers had long sailed the Irish Sea, using the Isle of Man as a base, but with the acquisition of that island by the Crown in 1765 the smugglers' bases shifted to the Channel Islands and the French coast, and Pembrokeshire, formerly peripheral to their operations, now became first port of call on journeys north. New markets meant new and more cargoes!

There were wreckers a'plenty too around the coast — not only wreckers lighting beacons on lonely headlands, as reported by local historian Richard Fenton about Llanunwas near Solva, but also local farmers and fishermen who plundered any wrecks, selling cargoes and plunder for food, and often saving crew's lives. In 1754 the *Margaret*, en route in ballast from Dublin to Cork, parted company from her anchor in St Brides Bay, her crew taken to the lifeboat drowned, and the ship wrecked on Druidston cliffs. The Customs guard of 30 men was insufficient to prevent the local population from tearing the ship apart with hatchets.

Piracy was not unknown. John Paul Jones, the American privateer, paid a visit during the War of Independence, his *Black Prince* firing a couple of broadsides at Lower Fishguard as an incentive for the ransom of a merchant vessel he had captured. Pembrokeshire exported one famous pirate. Born Bartholomew Roberts at Little Newcastle, near Fishguard, in 1682, he became the terror of the Spanish Main, commanding his own vessel from 1719 until his death in 1722. He became known as Black Bart, or *Barti Ddu*. The French, however, admiring his red coat, his black flag with skull and hourglass, and the fact that he sailed with an orchestra on board, gave him another name, '*Le Joli Rouge*' — the original 'Jolly Roger'.

It was not until the late 17th century that the Customs Board began to patrol the English and Welsh coasts, with at least 4 cutters being associated with Milford Haven by 1704. The 1st Revenue cutter known to be based in Milford Haven was the *Cardigan*, dating from 1757. At 60 tonnes she was equipped with 4 to 6 guns, with a crew of probably 12. Records note midnight chases across St Brides Bay in pursuit of incoming smugglers! By the beginning of the 19th century there were 12 cutters, but by 1850, following tariff reforms, numbers were drastically reduced. The smugglers responded by unloading cargo directly from their ships onto waiting local vessels and fishing boats for dispersed and safer landings. The last chase and arrest of a smuggler by a Milford based cutter was by the *Adder* in 1853 in the Caldey Roads, whiskey the cause of the trouble. Since then both smugglers and Customs have become more sophisticated — though the Customs seem to be winning smuggling still occurs around the coast even today!

★ ★ ★

3. Great views of St Brides Bay and the islands of Skomer and Ramsey. Druidston Haven (nothing to do with Druids, but one 12th century knight, Drue or Drew), right, has a fine sandy beach, it's isolation making it a fine alternative to more crowded Broad Haven. Inland to the north stands Roch Castle, guardian of the Landsker; to the south, around the corner from Little Haven, Talbenny church. On clear days good views of Grassholm Island, 7 miles/11 kilometres west of Skomer, and home to some 35,000 pairs of gannets, making it the 3rd largest colony in the world. Cliff erosion has always been a problem along this stretch of coast. Rock falls, isolated stacks and scree all mean less land for walkers, and more negotiations with local landowners for new diversions! Black Point's Iron Age fort, en route, is clearly in danger of slipping into the waiting sea. At both Newgale and Nolton Haven to the north, and at Little Haven, Broad Haven's sister village, there are significant coal and anthracite measures. Mining at Newgale and Nolton dates back to the 15th century — there were 6 main collieries, with Trefran perhaps the most important, in

operation from 1850 to 1905. The chimney stack, tramway track and ruined buildings are still extant, set among the cliffs north of Nolton Haven. Little Haven, very much a Cornish style village, owes much of it's development to the exploitation of coal, and acted as an important harbour for it's export, loading directly from beach to boat. Now a popular village, with fishing boats for hire.

Walk Directions: [-] denotes Point of Interest

1. Starting from the National Park car park in Broad Haven [1] take the path signposted 'Woodland Walk' to the left of the National Park Information Centre.

2. Go straight ahead, bearing slightly left behind the Coastguard Rescue vehicle building.

3. Bear right at a stile, and avoiding entrances for the Caravan Park, cross another stile to join a narrow path with a stream to your left.

4. Continue on the path through Haroldston Wood. After a short distance there is a path leading left up steps to the minor road between Broad Haven and Haroldston West, and marked 'Footpath'. Continue right, through the woodland.

5. Again after a short distance there is a path leading left to the minor road. Continue on the path bearing right.

6. At Timber Hill holiday chalets entrance continue straight ahead uphill, and where the path meets another path in front of Haroldston West church bear left, cross a stile, and join the minor road from Broad Haven at Haroldston West [2].

7. Bear right on the minor road, and continue straight ahead until the minor road leading left to Druidston Haven is reached.

8. Bear left towards Druidston Haven, passing between 2 stone pillars, until the 2nd cattle grid is reached. Bear left just past the grid to join the Coast Path — the route is signposted.

9. Continue on the path to cross a stile giving access to the coast [3].

10. Continue on the Coast Path to Broad Haven.

11. At the minor road turn right, cross the road bridge, and then immediately turn left onto a concrete path leading back to the National Park car park and the starting point. Signpost here, marked with a walking man, and indicating youth hostel and Information Centre.

Facilities:

Parking also possible by Haroldston West church.

All facilities available in Broad Haven — Broad Haven youth hostel has facilities for the disabled.

St Brides Haven - Nab Head - Tower Point - Musselwick Sands - Marloes - St Brides Castle - St Brides Haven

OS Maps:	1:50 000 St David's and Haverfordwest 157; 1:25 000 Outdoor Leisure 36 South Pembrokeshire/Haverfordwest (Hwlffordd) 1079 (SM 81/91), Skomer Island 1102 (SM 70).
Start:	Coast Path at St Brides Haven.
Access:	St Brides Haven can be reached from the B4327 Haverfordwest to Dale road, or on the minor roads from Little Haven and Broad Haven, and Marloes. Buses 315/316 operate from Haverfordwest to Marloes twice weekly on Tuesdays and Fridays only.
Parking:	St Brides Haven — in front of St Bridget's church.
Grade:	Easy — mainly coastal path and field.

Points of Interest:

1. St Brides Haven is a pretty little cove set in amongst the Old Red Sandstone cliffs of St Brides Bay. St Brides takes it's name from the popular 6th century Irish saint Bridget of Kildare. St Bride's popularity may have been helped along by association with the Celtic fertility goddess Brigantia. Whatever the connection St Bride was nominated as midwife to the Virgin Mary, and there was a chapel dedicated to St Bride here. The chapel stood service in later years as a herring salting house for local fishermen, before being washed into the sea. It is possible to pick out the stone remains of 2 coffins in the eroded cliffs by the sandstone limekiln. The present church dates from the 12th/13th century. There was a full restoration in 1868. It is a good example of the Celtic style —

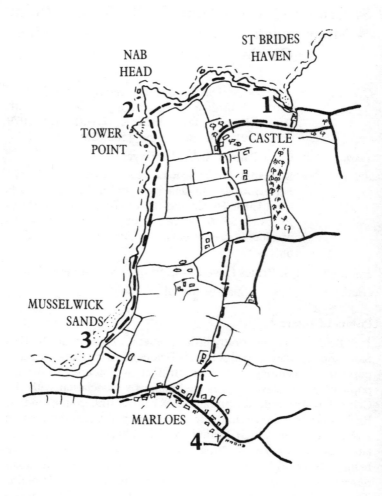

NAB
HEAD

ST BRIDES
HAVEN

2

TOWER
POINT

CASTLE

1

MUSSELWICK
SANDS

3

MARLOES

4

the Celtic crosses add an authentic touch, even if they are modern!

St Brides estate, to which the boundary wall remains, at one time belonged to the Barons of Kensington, whose Pembrokeshire lands stretched unbroken from St Brides to Haverfordwest. It was William Edwardes, Lord Kensington, who built the splendid St Brides Castle circa 1800 on the site of a former residence. With the break up of the estate the crenellated mansion became Kensington Hospital, specialising at various times as a convalescent home, a children's TB home, and between 1950-1970, as a geriatric hospital. With the opening of Withybush Hospital at Haverfordwest it became redundant; it was sold, and is now the Pembrokeshire home of the Holiday Property Board, offering luxury holiday apartments.

2. Nab Head derives it's name from knap i.e. the process of chipping flakes off flint. During the Mesolithic (8000 — 3000 BC) and Neolithic (3000 — 1800 BC) periods there was a movement away from cave dwelling to more open settlement. Whilst Mesolithic peoples tended to rely on hunting and fishing, the later Neolithic immigrants tended towards primitive cultivation and stock breeding. Yet both peoples, often existing side by side, required tools. Flint implements were mounted in bone or antler shafts, or occasionally wood, to make weapons, harpoons and simple tools. Eventually the 2 cultures began to merge. Excavations here have revealed the site to be a Mesolithic/Neolithic flint chipping factory. Axe and arrow heads, simple tools, as well as beads, have been found, and are on show in Tenby museum. Flint itself is not indigenous to the county; it may have been imported from Ireland, or carried down by northern ice sheets. It is quite probable that artefacts made on site were traded along the ancient trackways to other parts of Britain, and out by sea from St Brides Haven. Adjoining Tower Point has a later Iron Age fort, protected by a massive inner, and a smaller outer bank.

3. Musselwick Sands, tucked away out of reach of the prevailing south westerlies, has a fine sandy beach. Good swimming, and fewer crowds than at the better known Marloes Sands, the latter

one of the finest and most picturesque beaches in Wales. Beware of being cut off by an incoming tide, these are not the cliffs to climb in a hurry! At the beginning of the Mesolithic era Musselwick would have been well inland, but with the demise of the great northern ice fields the peats, woods and marshes favoured by Mesolithic hunters vanished slowly under the sea. The soft red sandstones fell victim, while the hard volcanic rocks of the Deer Park and St David's Head stood resistant, and remain to frame St Brides Bay. From Nab Head onwards the soft reds and purples mingle with black shales, until the uniform black of the rocky path down to Musselwick confirms the change to harder rock.

4. Marloes has the distinction of being the most westerly village in Wales. From here the road leads only to the Deer Park. Never mind that the Deer Park never held deer, it's prime conservation and landscape value; choughs and seals are the common residents, has led to it's designation as a Site of Special Scientific Interest (SSSI). From Martins Haven, Marloes' harbour, boats leave for the islands of Skomer and Skokholm, home to one of the great bird shows of Britain. Don't miss it! At one time Marloes fishermen sailed out to camp on Grassholm's gannet island in search of lobster and crayfish. Sea birds provided good bait; and eating. Conservation has somewhat changed the menu for all concerned! Marloes Mere, near the youth hostel, used to provide wildlife of a different kind. 19th century villagers used to stir the waters, and net that gruesome medical remedy to all problems — the leech. They were popular, at least, in Harley Street.

Marloes derives it's name from the Welsh, moel rhos, i.e. bare moor. Yet despite it's name it shows similarity in layout with English villages. The local church, St Peters, was restored in the 1870s. One noticeable architectural feature is the clock tower, built in 1904 by Lady Kensington, widow of William, the 4th Lord Kensington, who died in 1896. A plaque on the tower notes it as having been erected by members of the Pembrokeshire Liberal Association. It is said to have been built as a reminder of Lord Kensington's punctuality! As Barons of Kensington the Edwardes family noted their Pembrokeshire interests on the London map;

Marloes Road vies with Edwardes Square, Pembroke Road with Nevern Place. Under influence from Lord Kensington the village pubs were closed in the 19th century, and the village remained dry until 1963. Nowadays you will find plenty to wash down the excellent local seafood.

Walk Directions: [-] denotes Point of Interest

1. Start from the parking area in front of St Bridget's church in St Brides Haven **[1]**. Cross the beach head/picnic area to join the Coast Path.

2. Follow the Coast Path to Nab Head **[2]**, and continue on to Musselwick Sands **[3]**. For part of the way the Coast Path skirts the former St Brides estate boundary wall.

3. At Musselwick Sands take the path leading uphill left and inland, following the course of the stream. The route is well signposted. After a short distance the path turns to the right, leaves the stream, and enters an open field. Follow the left field edge to a stile.

4. Cross the stile, turn left, and follow the minor road into Marloes village **[4]**.

5. At the Lobster Pot pub (on your right as you walk), keep the Moriah Baptist chapel on your left, and turn left into Glebe Lane. Walk through the white kissing gate belonging to 'The Fold' — it is almost directly in front of you — and cross the property to reach an iron kissing gate leading into a field.

6. Cross the field, keeping to the field edge, and join a farm track through another kissing gate. Turn right.

7. At 'The Old School' leave the track through a wooden kissing gate. There is an old village pump opposite the gate.

8. Continue across fields, keeping to the edge. Halfway down the 3rd field there are stone steps set in the hedge which lead up to a stile. Signposted 'Public Footpath'. Cross this stile and turn right to join a farm track.

9. Follow the farm track downhill to where it forms a T junction with another farm track. Turn right.

10. Now look for a stile on your left — you will need to cross here quite shortly. After crossing keep to the right edge of the field and walk uphill to reach a stile. Cross the stile via the stone steps. St Brides Castle will now be in view.

11. Cross 3 fields to reach the stile leading into St Brides Castle grounds. Turn left and follow footpath signs and yellow waymarks through the grounds.

12. From the entrance to St Brides Castle, marked by a wooden walkers' gate and cattle grid, follow the access road until St Bridget's church is directly to your left. Turn left — you should be by a second cattle grid — and follow the path to the church gates, and via the church grounds back to the starting point.

Facilities:

Parking also possible in Marloes.

Public toilets and BT telephone at St Brides Haven; public toilets, Post Office and shop, BT telephone, and pubs in Marloes. There are guest houses in Marloes, and a youth hostel and camping sites nearby. Martins Haven is the embarkation point for boats to Skomer, Skokholm and Grassholm; there is an information board giving details of sailings to the islands on site — further details from Information Centres or Dale Sailing Company (01646 601636). The 1 mile/1.5 kilometre circuit of the Deer Park offers an additional short walk. Car park at Martins Haven — also Dyfed Wildlife Trust's Lockley Lodge and public toilets.

Dale - Dale Point - Castlebeach Bay - Watwick Bay - West Blockhouse Point - Mill Bay - St Ann's Head - Kete - Westdale Bay - Dale

OS Maps:	1:50 000 St David's and Haverfordwest 157; 1:25 000 Outdoor Leisure 36 South Pembrokeshire/Milford Haven 1103 (SM 80/90), Skomer Island 1102 (SM 70).
Start:	Dale
Access:	Dale is 11 miles from Haverfordwest on the B4327, and is within easy reach of Broad Haven and Little Haven, and St Brides Haven and Marloes. Buses 315/316 operate from Haverfordwest to Dale Tuesdays and Fridays only.
Parking:	There is a County Council car park in Dale — small seasonal charge. Very limited parking in the village.
Grade:	Moderate — a little road walking, but mostly coastal path.

Points of Interest:

1. Dale's written history begins in 1293 when a Robert de Vale was granted a charter to hold a weekly market and an annual fair. The present castle, a private residence, probably occupies the original castle's site. The medieval church, with it's 15th century tower, is dedicated to St James, and was substantially restored in the 1890s. By Tudor times Dale was a place of some importance, certainly so far as the Milford Haven is concerned Dale and Angle, on the opposite shore, were the largest villages, with Dale vying with Fishguard for size. Three 8 to 9 ton trading ships were owned, and Dale became known in Liverpool and Bristol for it's fine ale.

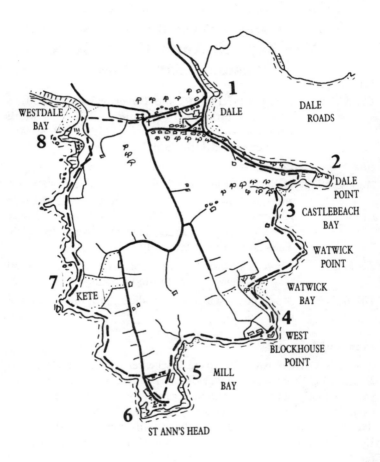

1 DALE

DALE ROADS

WESTDALE BAY

8

2 DALE POINT

3 CASTLEBEACH BAY

WATWICK POINT

WATWICK BAY

7 KETE

4 WEST BLOCKHOUSE POINT

5 MILL BAY

6

ST ANN'S HEAD

Fortunes seem to have declined by the 1800s however, with the village fallen into ruins, but by the 1850s 2 ships totalling 43 tons had been built, and fishing, shipbuilding and general trading were again to the fore. Whilst Dale is noted as the sunniest place in Wales, the Dale peninsula makes up for it by being one of the windiest in Britain! Dale's forté is now water sports, though there is still good ale to be had! Often used as an overnight anchorage by ocean going yachts, Dale Roads played host to many of the finest sailing ships in the world during the Tall Ships race in 1991.

2. There was an Iron Age fort here by 300 BC — the single bank and ditch are clearly visible, running out across the headland from between the 2 stiles, with the former entrance in the middle of the bank. Dale Fort was built as part of Milford Haven's 19th century defensive system between 1852 and 1856, the road leading to it from Dale being the old military access road. The fort was taken over in 1947 by the Field Studies Council who run courses mainly in marine biology, though geology, geography, archaeology and painting also find a place. Good views from the headland over Dale Roads. The small cove of Monk Haven, across the water, was a favourite landing place during the Age of the Saints and the Middle Ages, with travellers and pilgrims preferring to use the old Neolithic and Bronze Age trackway from Monk Haven as a safe route to St David's, thus avoiding the hazards of the sea. The sandstone wall across the head of the beach, just visible, was built in the 18th century as an estate boundary. Clearly visible around the coast here are the layers of Old Red Sandstone which underlie most of the Milford Haven area.

3. Castlebeach is a pleasant wooded bay with a sandy beach. There is an old limekiln at the head of the beach where limestone quarried at West Williamston, near Lawrenny, or on Caldey Island, would have been burnt to provide lime for local farms as fertilizer or mortar. Now overgrown there are the ruins of the lime burner's cottage in the wood. Lime burning had largely died out by the beginning of the 20th century, the last recorded use of kilns in the Dale area was at Pickleridge in the 1920s.

4. West Blockhouse Point derives it's name from the Victorian fort built here as part of Milford Haven's fortifications. The first attempt to fortify the Haven was undertaken by Henry VIII, with blockhouses on both northern and southern sides of the Haven entrance, but of these only that at Angle survives. Further fortifications had to wait until the mid 19th century when fears of French invasion led to a more thorough system. West Blockhouse was matched by another fort, now demolished, on the opposite shore, by Rat Island at East Angle; Dale Fort was matched by the island fort on Thorn Island; the circular island fort on Stack Rock by Popton Fort, at Angle Bay; and so on down the Haven, until the Defensible Barracks, holding the main defence force of 500 men, was reached at the new Royal Naval Dockyard at Pembroke Dock. The whole system, complete by 1875, was overseen by General Gordon of Khartoum fame. Obsolete as soon as built, and without a shot having been fired, these forts became known as Palmerston's Follies — after Palmerston, at various times Prime Minister and Foreign Secretary during mid century. The fort here was built by 1857 for 80 men, and was at last utilized during both World Wars, for anti-aircraft defence. By 1950 the fort was abandoned, and is now the property of the Landmark Trust, in use for holiday letting.

The 3 navigation towers, together with that on Watwick Point, were built in 1970. By holding the central tower here in transit with that on Watwick Point, shipping is led into the deep water channel. There is a similar system of buildings and towers on Great Castle Head for the next deep channel section. The Master of the vessel simply aligns the lights, or the white or black lines. At night the lights have a possible range of 19 miles/30 kilometres, the red lights on the 2 outer towers here indicating the channel entrance. Watwick Point tower currently ranks as the 3rd tallest lighthouse in the world. They are under the jurisdiction of the Milford Haven Port Authority.

5. Mill Bay, just before sunset on Sunday, 7 August 1485, was the unlikely host to the beginnings of one of the great adventures of British history, when, like so many young dragons, Henry Tudor

came ashore from Brittany with 2000 men, to begin his lightning march to Stafford, Bosworth Field, and the English crown. Born in nearby Pembroke Castle in 1459, Henry had been left sole heir to the Lancastrian throne following the Wars of the Roses, and had had to seek refuge in France. Recalled in 1485 Henry landed on home territory to meet enthusiastic support, many hailing him as the new King Arthur. By 22 August Richard III was dead, the Tudor age inaugurated, and Henry VII on the throne.

The wreck here is that of a boom defence vessel which broke away from the tug towing it for scrap in 1964. One earlier disaster from the days of sail — the Mill Bay Disaster — occurred in September 1866. The leader of a group of 6 or 7 sailing ships running before a gale in poor visibility went aground — the others followed suit with disasterous loss of life.

6. There was once a small chapel here, dedicated to St Ann, mother of Mary and patron saint of Brittany, and quite possibly established by Henry VII in thanks for his victory at Bosworth Field. There was a 20 feet/6 metres high tower light attached to the chapel, a great boon to ships entering the Haven. However the chapel was demolished during the Reformation, though the tower light was rebuilt. A second lighthouse was built in 1714, which comprised 2 towers lit by coal. The front tower was rebuilt further inland in 1841, and was modernised in 1958 when it was put onto electricity. The rear light became the Coastguard station in 1910. The small tower house contains the foghorn. The old Coastguard and Trinity House cottages and the Coastguard station are now in private ownership. The walled garden and stone quay nearby date from 1800, the latter built for transporting materials for the lighthouse. A new thin steel towered lighthouse was built out at sea, just off the Head, in 1966, to mark the entrance to the deep water channel — the Mid Channel Rocks Lighthouse.

The area between St Ann's Head, across to the Angle peninsula and flat topped Linney Head, is known locally as 'The Heads'. Some 100,000 years ago the Bristol Channel was mostly land, and the river then flowing through the Haven would have continued across the plain to join the Severn almost halfway between St Ann's Head and Lands End in Cornwall, but with the end of the Ice Age the meltwater flooded the Haven, creating a ria, or drowned river valley, much along present lines. The mouth of the Haven is 1.25 miles/2 kilometres wide, and 18 miles/30 kilometres long, navigable as far as Haverfordwest and Canaston Bridge. The decision to create a major oil port was taken in the late 1950s, Esso the first refinery to open in 1960. Some veritable giants of tankers are now common fare; however there are always some, inevitably, that seem to go astray. In October 1978 the Greek tanker *Christos Bitas* went aground on the Hats and Barrels reef, near Grassholm Island, spilling 35,000 tons of oil. As a result of this incident the Centre for Oiled Birds was established at West Williamston near Carew. The Centre was well occupied in February 1996 when the *Sea Empress* went aground on the shoals and rocks below St Ann's Head, spilling 70,000 tons of light crude oil in the 6 days it took to tow her off the rocks.

7. Great views from here of the islands of Skokholm, Grassholm and Skomer — life on this side of the peninsula is much quieter than the activity and bustle of the Haven. Ronald Lockley made Skokholm his island home from 1927 to 1939, establishing Britain's first bird observatory there in 1933. His 2 books, 'Dream Island' and 'Island Days', describe his life, where he "resolved to imitate [Thoreau's] austere mode of living when I at last came to dwell on my dream island". Together with Skomer and Grassholm these islands represent some of the finest seabird colonies in Europe, with shearwaters, gannets, razorbills, guillemots, choughs and the splendid puffins. They can be reached from Martins Haven, near Marloes. Kete was the site of HMS Harrier, a Royal Navy radar and meteorological school, which closed in 1960. The land was bought by the National Trust in 1967, buildings cleared, and the area returned to agricultural use. The former married quarters in Dale are now private residences.

8. Unlike Dale, Westdale Bay has a sandy beach, but beware of the strong undertow on the ebb tide if you are planning to swim.

Overlooking the bay on the south side is the Iron Age fort on Great Castle Head, dating from circa 100 BC. It has massive banks and ditches, and is particularly impressive on the approach from Kete. The entrance makes good use of the rock faulting. To the north, again overlooking the bay, are the remains of the old Dale airfield, which was to transfer to Brawdy, near Newgale. The route from Westdale back to Dale follows the course of an old river valley, and, but for the fall in sea level, Dale peninsula would have remained an island.

Walk Directions: [-] denotes Point of Interest

1. Starting from Dale [1] walk past the Griffin Inn and Dale Yacht Club and follow the tarmac road to Dale Fort Field Centre.

2. Just before the Field Centre views open up, left, over Dale Roads. To the right 2 almost adjacent stiles give access to the coastal path and the headland overlooking Dale Point [2].

3. Follow the Coast Path from Dale Point on to Castlebeach Bay [3], and continue on past the navigation beacon on Watwick Point to the sandy beach of Watwick Bay — a popular bay in summer. Access to the beach down a narrow footpath.

4. Continue to West Blockhouse Point [4], and Mill Bay's small rocky inlet [5], to arrive at St Ann's Head, [6] guarding the entrance to the Milford Haven.

5. The tarmac road leads 2 miles/3 kilometres back to Dale — continue however the 2.5 miles/4 kilometres on the Coast Path around to Kete [7] and Westdale Bay [8].

6. From Westdale Bay — easy access to the beach down convenient steps — cross the stone stile to the right of the Coast Path, and continue inland across the centre of the field to join the farm track leading to Hayguard Hay Farm.

7. Continue ahead on the farm track to shortly join the road leading back into Dale and the starting point. Choice of road, or footpath across the fields by Dale car park.

Facilities:

Free parking in the National Trust car park at Kete — there is no official car parking at St Ann's Head. Limited parking also on the road leading from Maryborough Farm down towards West Blockhouse Point — a footpath and stile leads off from here to Watwick Bay. Limited parking is also possible in the parking bay above Westdale Bay — follow the road behind Dale Castle.

All facilities are available in Dale. A very popular centre for water sports.

Nant y Coy Mill (Wolf's Castle) - Great Treffgarne Rocks - Maiden Castle - Upper North Hill Farm - Nant y Coy Mill (Wolf's Castle)

OS Maps: 1:50 000 St David's and Haverfordwest 157; 1:25 000 Outdoor Leisure 35 North Pembrokeshire/ Newgale and Wolf's Castle 1056 (SM 82/92).

Start: Nant y Coy Mill

Access: Nant y Coy Mill is just south of Wolf's Castle on the A40 Fishguard to Haverfordwest road, and is 5.5 miles/9 kilometres from Haverfordwest, 8.5 miles/13.5 kilometres from Fishguard. Bus 412 stops at Wolf's Castle en route from Cardigan and Fishguard to Haverfordwest.

Parking: There is a good sized lay-by at Nant y Coy Mill.

Grade: Moderate — mainly field, farm and green lanes.

Points of Interest:

1. There has been a corn mill here, curled at the foot of Treffgarne gorge, since at least the early 14th century. With a major overhaul in 1844 the mill went on producing corn until the 1950s, when it became a working farm. From 1971 it has operated as a gift shop, tea-room and museum. The old mill wheel is still there, restored and tucked away behind the newly renovated buildings. Wolf's Castle is a Norman village, with the castle mound remaining from the old wooden motte and bailey castle which once stood here on the Landsker line, defending Normans from angry Welsh. The wolf in question may have been a visiting Viking by the name of Ulf. There is an attractive Celtic style church nearby consisting of a

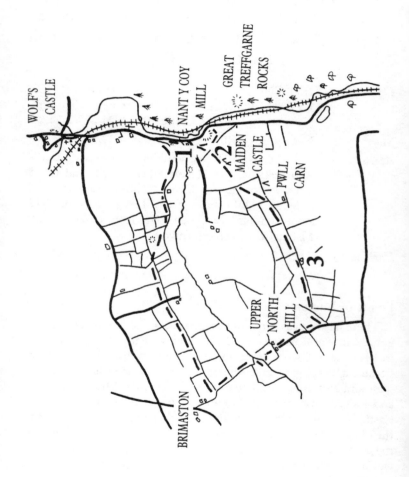

WOLF'S CASTLE

NANT Y COY MILL

GREAT TREFFGARNE ROCKS

MAIDEN CASTLE

PWLL CARN

UPPER NORTH HILL

BRIMASTON

2

3

single chamber, and, in the village, a Congregational chapel from 1807. The local pub fell victim to the Temperance movement in 1918, but was happily restored as the Wolfe Inn in 1964, offering good food and ale.

2. Great Treffgarne Rocks and the great tors of Maiden Castle and Pwll Carn form part of the igneous outcrops so prominent in the Pembrokeshire landscape. Like Carn Llidi and Pen Beri near St David's Head, Strumble Head and the Preselis, they have all weathered better than the softer more easily eroded sedimentary rocks with which they are surrounded. Treffgarne Rocks are among the oldest in the county — some 1,000 million years old — and these outliers of the Preseli range continue on almost to the coast with further carns at Plumstone and Roch. The gorge itself was cut by meltwater emptying from the Irish Sea glacier, which covered Pembrokeshire on at least 2 occasions 120,000 and 20,000 to 17,000 years ago. Legend has another explanation for the origins of the great tors. Discernible in the rocks of Maiden Castle are the shapes of a lion, bear and bear cub. It is said that the lion and the bear were fighting for possession of the cub, but were frozen in stone before the issue was resolved. There is another larger lion to be discerned in the shape of Pwll Carn, calmly overlooking events.

Iron Age man made good use of the natural landscape here. The rocks above the gorge were fortified with bank and ditch to make an impressive, well defensible fort. Outside the fort are traces of hut circles and fields, and the area as a whole was well settled with at least 12 settlements within easy reach of each other. Brunel, that great Victorian, was here in the late 1840s to add his touches to the landscape. He had ambitions to build a rail link to Ireland via a new harbour at Fishguard. Work began in earnest with levels being cut in the gorge which are still traceable today, on the far side of the present railway line. However the terrible Irish famine meant lack of investment and Brunel abandoned the workings in 1851 and took his line south to Neyland. A line was laid to Fishguard in 1899 — the North Pembrokeshire and Fishguard Railway — but this went by way of Maenclochog to the east. However it was unsuitable for fast traffic, and the present railway was built by the Great Western Railway to serve Fishguard Harbour, opened in 1908. Soon passengers direct from New York came hurtling through the gorge en route to London.

3. One of the finest views in the north of the county. To stand in the centre of the field is like being in the centre of a vast bowl, surrounded by the great igneous rock outcrops, the odd settlement or farm standing clear from the earth, with to the south the spikes of the oil refineries, and to the west the sea.

Walk Directions: [-] denotes Point of Interest

1. From Nant y Coy Mill [1] walk up the tarmac road, marked with a 'No Through Road' sign.

2. Just at the top of the rise there is a parking bay on the right, and a footpath left, indicated by a metal sign of a walking man.

3. Continue on the footpath. Almost immediately there is a path on the right leading to Maiden Castle. Continue straight on to shortly reach the rocks overlooking Treffgarne gorge [2].

4. From the gorge retrace your steps to the footpath leading to Maiden Castle, and ascend to the tor.

5. Keeping Maiden Castle to your left continue ahead to a stile. Cross the stile and continue diagonally left to the top left of the field to reach another stile.

6. Cross the stile into a second field, and keeping to the left field edge, continue over 2 more stiles to reach a 4th field. A short way past the last stile there is an OS trig point tipped over on it's side by the adjacent field fence [3].

7. Continue to a stile, adjacent to a farm gate, which gives access to a farm track. Turn left — right leads to Lower North Hill Farm.

8. Continue to a tarmac road, turn right, and follow it to Upper North Hill Farm.

9. At the farm turn right onto the track in front of the hedge and follow it around left into the farmyard. Continue ahead across a field to reach a stile.

10. Follow the path on through sallow trees and brambles to cross a small footbridge across Nant y Coy brook. Cross by another stile, go up a short rise, and turn and follow the right wooded field edge to another stile.

11. Cross this field, keeping to the left edge, to reach a green lane. Continue on the green lane to meet another lane leading to the right.

12. Continue right until the green lane meets the tarmac road to South Hill.

13. Continue ahead, up stone steps, and keeping to the right field edge, cross 2 fields to enter a 3rd field.

14. Turn immediately right and cross over another stile into a 4th field. Continue diagonally left to an earthwork, hedged with gorse, and then down a short rise to the top corner of the field to join a farm track.

15. Continue on the farm track to West Field Farm. Where the track bears right go ahead through a farm gate, and keeping the farm house on the right, rejoin the farm lane.

16. Continue on the farm lane to join the main A40. Turn right to return to the starting point.

Facilities:

Nant y Coy Mill is open Easter to mid October, and offers a craft shop and tearoom, as well as exhibitions of local history. Free entry! Wolf's Castle has a pub, a hotel, shop and Post Office and BT telephone.

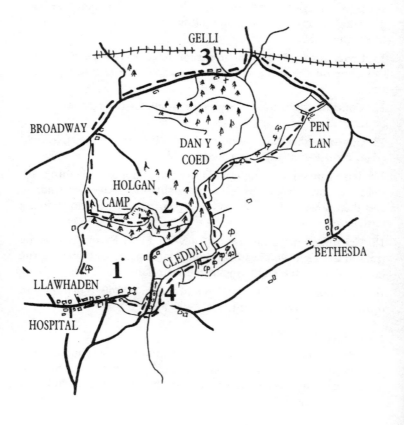

Llawhaden - Broadway - Gelli - Pen Lan - St Aidan's Church - Llawhaden

OS Maps:	1:50 000 Tenby 158; 1:25 000 Outdoor Leisure 36 South Pembrokeshire/Narberth (Arberth) 1080 (SN 01/11)
Start:	Public footpath, signposted 'Holgan Camp 1 Mile', in Llawhaden — adjacent to BT telephone kiosk.
Access:	Llawhaden is 1.5 miles/2.5 kilometres from the A40 Haverfordwest to St Clears main road, at the junction of the A40 with the A4075 at Canaston Bridge. Canaston Bridge is on the main bus route from Haverfordwest to Carmarthen and Narberth. Bus 392 stops at Llawhaden Fridays only. Buses 322/323 and 381 pass the turn-off to Llawhaden.
Parking:	Llawhaden — parking areas near the castle, or in front of the medieval hospital.
Grade:	Moderate — some road walking, otherwise mostly field and woodland paths, and green lane.

Points of Interest:

1. During the Norman period the largest diocese in Wales was that of St David's. To reflect its considerable wealth and prestige bishop's palaces were built at St David's, Lamphey, Trefin and Llawhaden. Bernard, elected as first Norman bishop of St David's in 1115, built an earth and timber ringwork here, but this was raised to the ground in 1192 by Prince Rhys, who was intent on reclaiming land he had lost to the Normans. The second castle was built in stone by Bishop Thomas Beck (1280-1293) and his successor Bishop David Martin (1293-1327). It became a fortified residence, set around a courtyard. A gatehouse was added in the

14th century. The residence, on its superb location commanding views of the Preselis and eastern Cleddau, remained in favour until partially dismantled by Bishop Barlow (1536-1547) at the time of the Reformation. One reason for its literal fall from grace was that the reverent bishop needed to make good part of the dowry for one of his daughters!

It was Bishop Beck who transformed the settlement of Llawhaden, refounding it as a medieval borough with extensive burgage tenements (i.e. rented property). In 1287 he founded a hospital and hospice in the village for pilgrims and paupers, dedicating it to St Mary. Though the hospital was later dissolved by Bishop Barlow in the mid 16th century, the chapel still survives. With typical Norman thoroughness the village was settled with English incomers, who alone were allowed to trade. The district was effectively divided in 2, with separate courts for English and Welsh. By the early 14th century the village was larger than St David's; however fortunes from hereon declined, until the village was revitalised by gentry families in the 17th and 18th centuries.

2. Holgan Camp is an Iron Age fort built on the site of an earlier Bronze Age settlement. One of many such forts in the area it's round beehive dwellings would have been defended by earthbanks, ditches and timber fence. Only the site now remains, with a high earthbank to one side. Great views of Llawhaden Castle, with the river snaking out far below towards St Aidan's church.

3. The present village of Gelli developed in the late 19th century around its woollen mill. At its height it was one of the largest in Pembrokeshire, employing some 30 workers. The mill was destroyed by fire in 1938. One architectural feature of Pembrokeshire villages, particularly those north of the Landsker like Gelli, are the chapels. Built out of funds raised by subscription from local people they are nearly all of a similar plan — rectangular buildings, with little furniture or ostentation. Only the wealthier chapels could afford a graveyard.

Landsker

Possibly Norse in origin for frontier, the term Landsker has been used to help define the frontier which emerged with the invasions of the Normans into Pembrokeshire. With the death of the last Prince of South Wales, Rhys ap Tewdwr, in 1093, came the Norman war machine to take his lands. By the end of the year Roger of Montgomery had taken South Pembrokeshire. Under constant Welsh attack the occupation of the new lands was consolidated, if a little haphazardly; and defended by a series of forts, later to become stone castles. The frontier line stretched from Roch in the west, to Wiston, Llawhaden, Narberth, Amroth, Laugharne and Llanstephan (Llansteffan).

The Norman pattern of the town and manorial village was established, the village often around a central green for defence, with grouped dwellings and farmhouses, a fortified manor house or castle, and a church and parsonage. Later the church acquired a high crenellated tower as lookout and last defence against encroaching Welsh. Requiring extra labour to administer the area led to the importation and settlement of Flemings, Saxon, and English, often in the Landsker zone. The creation of 'Little England beyond Wales' had begun.

North of the Landsker the landscape stayed true to the Celtic pattern, with isolated farms and villages, often divided by irregular stone wall boundaries, simple towerless churches with bellcotes, and few castles. The language remained firmly Welsh. By the 13th century the Landsker had ceased to have military significance, yet it was to remain a cultural divide — patterns of life and landscape that can be traced today.

* * *

Many date from the non conformist religious revivals of the 1730s and the late 1800s, when individual and collective religious experience was at its height. Nearby Bethesda's chapel dates from 1796, Gelli's from 1858. Characteristic was the evident language divide north and south of the Landsker. North the preachers and congregations thought, spoke, and sang in Welsh; south the language was English, the non conformism less widespread, and it's preachers more likely to be visiting Englishmen like John Wesley. A class and national consciousness is evident in the perception by the Welsh chapel goers of the church being English and Tory, allied with the landowners. The chapels were seen as radical and democratic; stern, but Welsh.

4. Llawhaden is a corruption of Llanaidan, literally the settlement or church of St Aidan. St Aidan is believed to be an Irish follower of St David, who later returned to Ireland, becoming the first Bishop of Ferns. The original church was of wood, probably dating from sometime between the 5th and 8th centuries. It was Bishop Beck who rebuilt it in stone in the 13th century. Substantial rebuilding was again needed in the 19th century. Set into the outside of the rear of the church wall facing the Cleddau is a stone slab, with underneath a projecting rock. The slab is believed to be a stone coffin lid, with it's Celtic cross worn off. It was the fashion during the Victorian restoration of churches to set a cross slab into the exterior of church walls. Could the stone slab underneath be the suggestion of a pilgrim's altar, like the Pilgrim's Cross at Nevern in North Pembrokeshire? At one time a cattle fair was held by Llawhaden's splendid bridge, rebuilt by the Skyrme family in the 18th century.

Walk Directions: [-] denotes Point of Interest

1. Start in Llawhaden [1]. Take the footpath adjacent to the BT telephone kiosk, marked 'Holgan Camp 1 Mile'. If you are walking from the castle the footpath and kiosk will be found on the right as you walk towards the medieval hospital.

2. Follow the farm track for half a mile/0.75 kilometres to Broomhill Grove. From here follow the path right, leading downhill and crossing a stream by a footbridge.

3. If you are detouring to Holgan Camp [2] then you will now need to turn right, just before a derelict cottage. The route is signposted.

Follow the path, which shortly becomes a Forestry Commission track. Follow this track for half a mile/0.75 kilometres until the track bends left and then sharp right. Holgan Camp is above you and left. Just before the forestry track turns sharp right there are steps leading up, back and left to a stile at the camp entrance. After visiting the camp return to the main walk the way you came.

4. Continue from the Holgan Camp turn uphill and straight ahead to Broadway and the minor road. Signposted at the road as bridleway.

5. Turn right and continue on the road to Gelli [3]. Ignore the bridleway leading right just past the chapel and cross Gelli bridge. Avoiding the railway bridge turn right over another bridge, and continue to join the road from Maenclochog. Continue right, uphill, to Pen Lan.

6. At Pen Lan (just over the border in Carmarthenshire) turn right and cross the stile just before Pen Lan Farm entrance. The walk now joins the Landsker Borderlands Trail and is well waymarked.

7. Cross 3 fields. Cross into the 4th field and keeping Llawhaden Castle directly in front of you, bear diagonally right towards it. As you top the field rise St Aidan's church tower becomes visible to the left below the castle. Continue to the stile at the corner of the field.

8. Keeping to the right field edge, above woodland, continue across 2 fields downhill to join a path bearing right downhill to the river. Note: the Ordnance Survey maps (other than Outdoor Leisure) show the path as leading back inland to 'Trewynt'. However since the instigation of the Landsker Borderlands Trail the path has been diverted and follows the course of the river to St Aidan's church.

9. Continue, then, initially through woodland, and then open fields until Dan y Coed Farm appears to the right, and on the other side of the river.

10. Continue across open fields to enter woodland. From the woodland the path — the castle is now directly in front of you and above — crosses 2 more fields before meeting the minor road to

Llawhaden.

11. Turn right onto the minor road, cross the bridge and again turn right and continue towards the church **[4]**. Take the path left directly opposite the church entrance, marked 'Public Footpath'.

12. Continue uphill on the path into Llawhaden and back to the starting point.

Facilities:

Parking also possible in Gelli.

Post Office and shop, BT telephone in Llawhaden. BT telephone in Gelli. Other facilities, including pub, available in Robeston Wathen.

Blackpool Mill - Sisters' House - Minwear - Forest Lodge - Blackpool Mill

OS Maps:	1:50 000 Tenby 158; 1:25 000 Outdoor Leisure 36 South Pembrokeshire/Narberth (Arberth) 1080 (SN 01/11).
Start:	Public footpath at Blackpool Mill.
Access:	Blackpool Mill is 0.75 miles/1.25 kilometres from Canaston Bridge, which is at the junction of the A4075 with the A40 Haverfordwest to St Clears road. The turning to Blackpool Mill is just to the south of Canaston Bridge on the A4075. Canaston Bridge is on the main bus route from Haverfordwest to Carmarthen and Narberth. Buses 322/323, 381 and 392 (Fridays only) stop at Canaston Bridge. Bus 393 (PostBus) from Narberth to Landshipping passes Blackpool Mill and Minwear Woods daily except Sundays.
Parking:	Blackpool Mill — parking area in grounds.
Grade:	Moderate — mostly woodland paths and green lane.

Points of Interest:

1. The superb 4 storey Georgian corn mill dates from 1813, when it was built by Baron de Rutzen of nearby Slebech Hall. In use until the 1950s, the mill has now been fully restored, and is one of the finest examples of a water driven mill in the country. In its heyday boats regularly delivered cargoes of grain for milling. An advert in the *Pembrokeshire Herald* in 1850, advertising the mill for let, advises that 'vessels of 80 tons burthen could load and unload on the spot'. The mill offers other attractions now. As well as the working machinery there are exhibitions of prehistoric life, a 19th century wheelwright's shop, coracles and model engines, and an

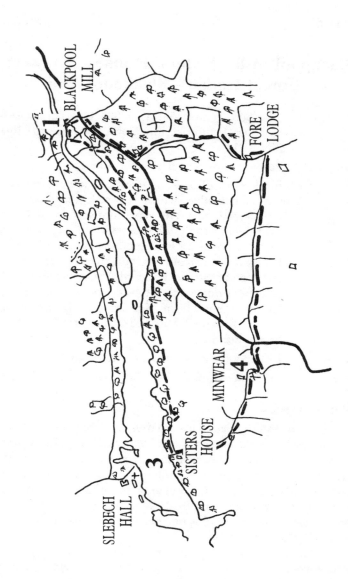

BLACKPOOL MILL

FORE LODGE

SLEBECH HALL

SISTERS HOUSE

MINWEAR

1

2

3

4

60

excellent shop and café. Open Easter to October 31. The attractive bridge across the Cleddau was erected circa 1830 by Baroness de Rutzen. Baron de Rutzen at one time introduced wild boar from Poland into nearby Canaston Wood for hunting. A similar scheme to introduce wolves met with stern opposition! Prior to the erection of the mill there was an important iron forge on the site, owned by the Carmarthen Iron Works. Products were domestic and agricultural equipment. Probably started as a small forge in the 16th century, by the 17th century both furnace and forge were in operation. Wood from Slebech Forest was used to fire the forge, whilst water power drove the massive hammers.

2. The extensive reed beds visible from the viewpoint survive at just the point where high spring tides penetrate. Any invasions of salt are quickly washed away by the downcoming river. A characteristic of the middle sections of estuarine rivers is the build up of wide mudbanks composed of silt; sediment deposited where the flows of saltwater and freshwater meet. Creatures which survive in the mud provide food for waders and wildfowl. The long beaks of curlew and godwit penetrate deep in the mud for lugworms; shelduck and wigeon select snails. In winter the concentrations of waders and duck prove attractive fare for birdwatchers, as do the duck for shooting parties.

Of Pilgrimages and Crusading Knights

A pilgrimage could encompass anything from a visit to a local shrine to a Crusade to the Holy Land, and could be undertaken by Kings and Queens, or by paupers. What made these medieval pilgrimages distinctive was the belief in the potency of a saint's relics. To touch or see the relics was to touch or see the saint; it eased suffering and brought health to the sick. From the 11th century onwards was added the belief that a pilgrimage could atone for previous sins.

Major pilgrimage sites were Rome and Jerusalem; with the alleged 9th century discovery of the tomb of St James the Apostle in northern Spain, Santiago de Compostela; and, locally, St David's. Naturally enough hospices and hospitals were established on the major pilgrimage routes and sites to cater for the pilgrims. With this aim in mind the Knights Hospitallers were first organised c.1070 at the Hospital of St John the Baptist in Jerusalem, predating the 1st Crusade of 1095-99 by some 20 years. Unlike Crusaders, who were seen as secular knights and pilgrims, the members of international military orders like the Knights Hospitallers and the Knights Templar (founded Jerusalem, 1118) were required to take vows permanently committing them to their order's ideals. Ideals of great piety; yet, as with the Crusaders, involving immense brutality against perceived non Christians. Truly Christian fundamentalism!

In 1198 the Knights Hospitallers established a Commandery at nearby Slebech, of which the church, although ruined, still stands on it's imposing position overlooking the eastern Cleddau. Well worth a visit! The Commandery was the organisation's Welsh headquarters, acting also as a hospital, a recruiting centre for the Crusades, and as a hospice for the pilgrim. Among local initiatives one by the then Bishop of St David's, Bishop Beck, led to the establishment of a hospital and hospice for pilgrims, travellers and the infirm in 1287 at Llawhaden, on one of the main routes to St David's. The chapel alone survives as testament to the popularity of the medieval pilgrimage. The Knights Hospitallers, unlike the Knights Templar, has survived the centuries, and owns both the ruined church at Slebech, and the land on which it stands.

* * *

Slebech Forest, of which Minwear Wood forms a part, is now managed by the Forestry Commission. In the late 18th century the forest was considered to be Pembrokeshire's most extensive wooded estate, encompassing both banks of the eastern Cleddau. Fortunately the Forestry Commission has allowed for a policy of mixed growth; conifers take the air along with beech, and a greater variety of wildlife interest is the result.

3. The ruins here are reputed to be those of the Sisters' House, a medieval hospice for female pilgrims on the way to St David's and St Non's Well. Directly opposite are Slebech Hall, a splendid building already glimpsed from the path, dating from 1776, and, hidden amongst the trees, the ruined church of the Commandery of the Knights Hospitaller of the Hospital of St John of Jerusalem. Many people are familiar with the image of the Crusading knight, with his white mantle and red cross. This was the uniform of the Knights Templar, who reputedly kept hospice in nearby Templeton. The Knights Hospitaller wore a black mantle with white 8 pointed cross. Dating from 1198 all that now remains of the Commandery is the ruined church, which is reachable by public footpath from Blackpool Mill. No doubt it was to the Commandery that female pilgrims were ferried across the river, before continuing on their pilgrimage. In the 19th century a possible ceremonial sword was found, buried on one of the small river islands. Perhaps it had been placed there after the dissolution of the monasteries by Henry VIII, away from the eyes of the Tudor Saracen?

4. The church dates from the 12th century, with a later, probably 14th century, tower. It was extensively restored in 1874 by Baron de Rutzen. The font is fronted by 4 faces, probably those of the 4 Evangelists. At one time it saw service as a farm trough! The church, with Minwear Farm, adjacent, was given in 1150 to the Knights Hospitaller, and formed part of their considerable estates in the county. Much of the land on the southern bank was cultivated by them, and most of their supplies came from here and nearby Martletwy, ferried across the river. It was proposed in the 15th century to build a causeway across the river, however there is nothing to show that it was ever begun.

Walk Directions: [-] denotes Point of Interest

1. Start from the parking area in Blackpool Mill **[1]** grounds. As you face the mill this is to your left, adjacent to the toilet block. From Blackpool Mill until Minwear the walk follows the Landsker Borderlands Trail and is well waymarked.

2. Cross diagonally right across the small field behind the toilet block to a wooden gate leading into a field.

3. Cross the second field, bearing diagonally left, to a stile.

4. Cross the stile and bear left, crossing a footbridge over boggy ground, and cross another stile onto a woodland path.

5. Almost immediately turn right through a wooden gate. There is a Forestry Commission post here, marked with a blue ring and a directional arrow. Follow the direction of the arrow i.e. go straight ahead, on a clearly defined path. You are now in Slebech Forest.

6. Continue on the footpath. After a quarter mile/0.5 kilometres there is a Forestry Commission path bearing left, and another blue ringed post. Opposite the turning there are 2 signs, 1 pointing back to Blackpool Mill, the other forward and marked 'Viewpoint'. Ignore the path left as this will take you to the road, and continue straight on.

7. The 'Viewpoint' in question is just ahead, and is signposted, indicating right turn. The very short detour here is recommended — the open views of the river are ample reward [2].

8. Return to the path and turn right, continuing in the original direction.

9. A short way further on there is again a Forestry Commission path and post, indicating left turn to the road. Continue straight ahead on the narrower footpath. Clearly defined by yellow waymarks. There is a fine, newly erected footbridge en route, bridging a local stream.

10. The path carries on unhindered for nearly a mile/1.5 kilometres, before making a slight diversion left at a field, where it continues downhill into woodland and turns right again to the river, crossing a stream on the way.

11. The path shortly meets a stile and wooden railings. Cross the stile and continue left. The ruins are those of the Sisters' House [3].

12. Cross the stile at the end of the fenced path to enter a wooded lane. Immediately enter the open field to the right of the lane and

keeping to the left edge of this field continue to the head of the field to join a farm track with a pond on the right.

13. Follow the track through Minwear Farm to join a tarmac road. Continue on this road past the church [4]. Ignore the stile on the right — the walk here parts company with the Landsker Borderlands Trail. Continue instead to the junction with the minor road between Blackpool Mill and Martletwy. Bear right and almost immediately turn left to join a bridleway, marked by a metal post and sign.

14. Continue straight ahead on the bridleway for a mile/1.5 kilometres, bearing left where the path forms a T junction with a farm track. Continue on this path, past 'Forest Lodge' on the right, to enter woodland. Follow the woodland track down to the minor road.

15. At the road bear right and follow the Forestry Commission track which fringes the road.

16. Where the Forestry Commission track joins the road continue along the road to Blackpool Mill and the starting point.

Facilities:

Parking also possible at Minwear.

Seasonal café and toilets at Blackpool Mill. No other facilities; nearest at Robeston Wathen. Landshipping, on the river south of Minwear, has a good pub. Oakwood Leisure Park and Canaston Centre (Cyberdrome Crystal Maze and Ten Pin bowling) are close by, on the A4075 south from Canaston Bridge. Blackpool Mill is the start (or end) of the Knights' Way, a 9 mile/14.5 kilometre link path between the Cleddau and Amroth on Carmarthen Bay.

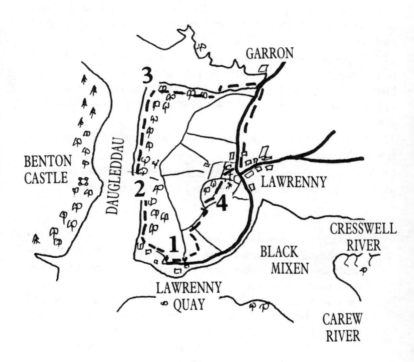

GARRON

BENTON CASTLE

DAUGLEDDAU

LAWRENNY

CRESSWELL RIVER

BLACK MIXEN

CAREW RIVER

LAWRENNY QUAY

Lawrenny Quay - Garron Pill
- Lawrenny - Lawrenny Quay

OS Maps:	1:50 000 Tenby 158, St David's and Haverfordwest 157; 1:25 000 Outdoor Leisure 36 South Pembrokeshire/Tenby & Saundersfoot 1104 (SN 00/10).
Start:	Public footpath at Lawrenny Quay.
Access:	Lawrenny can be reached from the A4075 Carew to Canaston Bridge road, either following the minor road from Creselly, or from Cross Hands near Oakwood Leisure Park. Just follow the Lawrenny signposts. PostBus 394 Narberth to Lawrenny operates daily except Sundays.
Parking:	Lawrenny Quay — by the Yacht Station.
Grade:	Easy — woodland path, road, and field.

Points of Interest:

1. For centuries the sea and inland rivers have served as a magical highway for Pembrokeshire trade, commerce and communication. Viking raiders penetrated the Milford Haven as far north as Haverfordwest, whilst embattled Normans took care wherever possible to build their castles not only on strategic sites, but also on sites that overlooked or had access to the waterways of the Haven and the Daugleddau. From the Middle Ages onwards cargoes of coal, limestone, timber and grain set out from and arrived at all ports of call on the river. In this atmosphere of bustle and activity Lawrenny's prosperity grew; it's quay was developed, and it's shipbuilding industry increased in importance.

At nearby West Williamston, across the water at the junction of the Carew and Cresswell rivers, channels had been cut to give barges of 15 to 20 tons access to it's limestone quarries. Often the barges carried their loads to Haverfordwest, but it was usual to transship them at Lawrenny. A significant coal measure extended in a narrow strip from Saundersfoot to Nolton, passing to the north of Lawrenny. Those collieries of the Daugleddau Coalfield adjacent to the river established small quays for export. When visiting ships outgrew these quays, as they did at Cresswell and Landshipping, it became customary for barges to take the coal to Lawrenny, or nearby Llangwm, for reloading into waiting ships. It was for this purpose that Lawrenny's quay had been developed. People, as well as cargoes, were constantly on the move from Lawrenny Quay. Ferries took people and their wares down to Cosheston ferry and across to Roose ferry. The last ferry service continued until the 1960s.

At one time Lawrenny's shipyard was second only to Milford Haven's. From the 1800s through to the 1850s Milford built 91 ships; whilst Lawrenny's total was 61. The building of new towns downriver; Milford Haven from the 1790s, Pembroke Dock from 1814, and Neyland as the railway terminus from 1856, together with larger ships, spelt the end of village trade and quays. There was no shipbuilding at Lawrenny after the 1850s. Lawrenny Quay now is a pleasant holiday site, catering to the boating and walking enthusiast, as well as the day tripper.

2. The Daugleddau (the 2 swords) is strictly speaking that part of the river from the Cleddau Bridge to Picton Point, where the western and eastern swords join. The Daugleddau, with it's many small creeks, or pills, are a series of drowned river valleys, or rias, formed at the end of the Ice Age. The woodland is semi-natural oak, with the occasional wild service tree. Deciduous woodlands are now a rarity in Pembrokeshire and are found mainly here, on the banks of the Daugleddau, or further north in the Gwaun valley, near Fishguard. Steep valley slopes have been their best defence against farming. Benton Castle, opposite, with its smart coat of whitewash, dates from the 13th century, reputedly built by Bishop

Beck of St David's. Substantially rebuilt in the 1930s, it is now a private residence.

3. Garron Pill is typical of the many small inlets on the river. From here the river's pattern of alternating low meadow land and steep wooded slopes abutting the shore becomes evident. The mudflats provide good feeding grounds for wildfowl and waders. Curlews, shelduck and teal compete with wigeon and mallard. The town of Llangwm, diagonally opposite, was famous in the 19th century for the quality of its oysters. There has been a recent attempt here to revive the industry by farming oyster beds on pontoons. These have been set at the mouth to the pill, allowing for access at low tide. The women of Llangwm were noted in the county and South Wales for their individualism. At one time they used to row their menfolk downriver to work at the new towns, returning later in the day to collect them. They had their own distinctive fashion, and travelled from town to village selling the local fish and oysters. The wooden hut, overlooking the pill, is used by the local scouts/guides. Coedcanlas, opposite, on Garron's side of the river, was the birthplace of Dick Francis, the author and jockey. There must be something in the local air — Lawrenny's stables produced a Grand National winner in 1905 with Kirkland!

4. Stunning views over Black Mixen below and the Carew and Cresswell rivers. The old limestone quarries at West Williamston opposite are now a nature reserve managed by the Dyfed Wildlife Trust. There have been 2 mansions here on this site. Early 18th century Lawrenny House was demolished to make way for Lawrenny Castle, a magnificent Victorian house dating from 1850, sadly demolished in the 1950s after failures to find a buyer. The castle became the officer's mess during the Second World War when the Navy arrived with a seaplane training squadron in 1941. Lawrenny soon echoed to the sounds of Kingfisher and Walrus seaplane engines. Lawrenny's fine church is the only one in the county dedicated to the 12th century Celtic saint Caradoc, who is known to have lived in Pembrokeshire. Originally late 13th century, a west tower was added in the 16th century.

Walk Directions: [-] denotes Point of Interest

1. Start from the car park by the Yacht Station in Lawrenny Quay [1]. Continue on the road to the boat park.

2. Immediately turn left and cross the boat park. At the track turn sharp left, and then sharp right to enter a wood.

3. Continue on the woodland track until, after a short distance, you reach a private house.

4. At the house turn right and continue on a well defined footpath to cross a wooden stile. There is a smart doggie stile here on your left, as well as a National Trust sign marked 'Lawrenny'.

5. Continue on the path. There are fine views from the path of Benton Castle opposite [2], before the path turns right inland by Garron Pill [3].

6. Continue on the woodland path, passing the scout/guides hut, to reach a stile on your left. Cross the stile and follow the steps down to the shore. Turn right and continue inland along the shore — beware of high tides!

7. At the minor road turn right and continue uphill to Lawrenny village.

8. Turn right into Lawrenny Picnic Site and Viewpoint and continue, with the church on your left, through stone pillars to the car park and picnic site [4]. The solitary lion guarding the entrance lost his brother when he was stolen in the 1960s!

9. Cross the picnic site to the top left hand corner — there is a viewpoint information panel here — and turn right to follow the top wall, which leads you down stone steps to cross a stile into a field.

10. Cross diagonally left to another stile almost in front of you.

11. Cross the stile, turn right, and keeping to the right field edge continue to another wooden stile.

12. Cross the stile, turn left and follow the farm track downhill through woodland as it bends left, and then right, to join the minor road into Lawrenny Quay.

13. Continue right on the road — you are now opposite the Lawrenny Arms — and back to the starting point.

Facilities:

Parking is also possible at Lawrenny Picnic Site and Viewpoint, and in Lawrenny village.

Lawrenny Quay offers the Lawrenny Arms Hotel. The public toilets by the hotel are open April to October only. BT telephone. Lawrenny village has a youth hostel, Activity Centre, a Post Office and BT telephone. Slipway at Lawrenny Yacht Station, which keeps some of its moorings for visitors. Also caters for boat engine repairs. Good pub, the Cresselly Arms, at nearby Cresswell Quay.

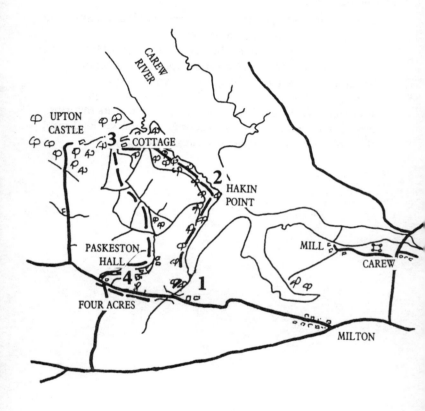

CAREW RIVER

UPTON CASTLE

3 COTTAGE

2 HAKIN POINT

PASKESTON HALL

4

1

FOUR ACRES

MILL

CAREW

MILTON

72

Ford Bridge - Hakin Point - Carew River - Paskeston Cottage - Paskeston Hall - Ford Bridge

OS Maps:	1:50 000 Tenby 158, St David's and Haverfordwest 157; Outdoor Leisure 36 South Pembrokeshire/1:25 000 Tenby & Saundersfoot 1104 (SN 00/10), Manorbier & Tenby (SS 09/19).
Start:	Ford bridge.
Access:	From the A477 Pembroke Dock to St Clears road take the minor road leading from Milton to Cosheston. The walk begins approximately 1 mile/1.5 kilometres away from Milton, 1.25 miles/2 kilometres from Cosheston. Buses 332/333 and 361 stop at Milton en route from Tenby to Pembroke Dock.
Parking:	There is a small lay-by on the left just before Ford bridge as you travel from Milton — also limited parking on the roadside verge opposite Four Acres.
Grade:	Easy — mostly woodland path, field and track. Be warned — the woodland section can be muddy in places!

Points of Interest:

1. The woodland here is mixed deciduous; plenty of sycamore, ash, beech and hazel, with oak and holly. During World War 2 the wood was coppiced and the timber taken out along much the same route as the present path — prisoners of war would have helped in the task. The woodland floor is initially carpeted by wild garlic, at it's best from April to June when the starlike white flowers are out on show. Snowberry soon takes over, edging the path for much of it's length.

2. In days gone by, when Carew French Tidal Mill was flourishing, steam barges and wooden sailing ships would have been seen heading up to the mill to deliver corn from Sandy Haven and other Milford Haven creeks, perhaps even from Bristol. The ground seed would have found local use. Nowadays the wide and shallow Carew river, home to curlew and shelduck, is only likely to play host to the occasional adventurous dinghy. There has been a mill upriver since at least 1541, and since restoration in 1972 it can be visited from April to September.

Whilst only the causeway to the mill can be seen from here, Carew Castle, in it's glorious strategic setting around the river bend, stands resplendent, guardian of the inner reaches. It is believed to have been founded by Gerald de Windsor, castellan of Pembroke from 1093 to 1116. There were various additions over the centuries until circa 1480 Gerald's descendants sold it to Sir Rhys ap Thomas who enhanced the building, and is famed as the giver, in 1507, of the last great medieval tournament of Britain. 5 days of feasting, harp music, and song were accompanied by contests of tilting, athletics, wrestling and deer hunting in the park, with evenings of theatricals and drinking. It is said a 1,000 men attended, and not a single fight or quarrel broke out!

On the impeachment of Sir Rhys's grandson the castle passed to Sir John Perrott, reputedly the son of Henry VIII. Lord Deputy of Ireland, and a Privy Councillor, he continued the castle's transformation into a brilliant Elizabethan palace, adding the superb North Gallery with it's mullioned windows. Turkish carpets, Irish rugs, silks, books and musical instruments and piped water were added to the interior. However before he could occupy it he was convicted of treason, and died in the Tower of London in 1592. After this great flowering the castle fell on hard times, suffering 2 sieges during the Civil War before falling into ruin. The castle is now open to the public April to September.

3. Paskeston Cottage, in ruins, was last occupied in the late 1930s. Whilst not visible from the path, opposite, on the other side of the creek, is Upton Castle, a minor stronghold dating from the 13th century. It is now a private residence. Though there is no access to

the castle from the path the extensive gardens are open most days April to September, and can be reached from the Milton to Cosheston road. Noted for it's fine collection of trees and shrubs.

4. Paskeston Hall, a traditional 3 storey house, dates from circa 1730. A hall was added in the mid 18th century. In private hands.

Walk Directions: [-] denotes Point of Interest

1. Starting from the lay-by cross Ford bridge and turn right onto a farm track.

2. Cross over a wooden stile on the right just before the farm gate. There is a footpath sign here, marked 'Public Footpath RA Jubilee Walk'. The walk was reinstated in 1985 on the 50th anniversary of the Ramblers Association.

3. Follow the clearly defined path through the woodland [1].

4. After a half mile/0.75 kilometres the path momentarily emerges from the woodland into a small reed bed, partly shaded by a large oak. Open views of the river and Carew Castle to the right [2].

5. The walk continues straight ahead, but it is worthwhile taking the very short detour on the less well defined path on the immediate right, just past the reed bed, to Hakin Point. Great views.

6. Continue on the main path, passing a limekiln on your right (lime was formerly required for sweetening Pembrokeshire's acid soil) to reach the wooden stile by the now ruined Paskeston Cottage [3].

7. Cross the stile, and leaving the woodland behind you, turn left. Go straight ahead up the wooded green lane to cross another stile into a field.

8. Cross the field, keeping to the left field edge, to cross another stile onto a farm track.

9. Continue on the farm track, passing a small wood, and then a house, on your left.

10. Where the main track bends left to Paskeston Hall [4] and the

Milton to Cosheston road turn right through a field gate, and avoiding the buildings, enter the field and keeping to the left edge continue to another farm gate.

11. Leave the field to join a short wooded path bending left to join the track to Paskeston Hall.

12. At the track to Paskeston Hall cross the stile, turn right, and follow the path to join the minor road.

13. Turn left at the minor road, and with the lodge house on your left, continue downhill to the starting point.

Facilities:

None — nearest at either Milton or Cosheston. Upton Castle gardens open most days April to September, dependent on weather and number of visitors — free entry. Carew Castle and Celtic Cross are 0.75 miles/1 kilometre from Milton on the A4075.

West Angle Bay - Chapel Bay - Angle Point - Angle - West Angle Bay

OS Maps: 1:50 000 St David's and Haverfordwest 157; 1:25 000 Outdoor Leisure 36 South Pembrokeshire/ Milford Haven 1103 (SM 80/90).

Start: West Angle Bay.

Access: Angle is reached on the B4320 from Pembroke, or via Castlemartin on the B4319. PostBus 396 operates Monday to Saturday, Pembroke Dock and Pembroke to Angle and return, once daily — however the morning bus stops at nearby Rhoscrowther for 3½ hours on the outward journey from Pembroke Dock!

Parking: Free car park at West Angle Bay.

Grade: Easy — coastal path and minor road.

Points of Interest:

1. West Angle Bay is pleasant and attractive, with lots of sand, and plenty of rock pools for the young explorer. Situated as it is at the mouth of the Haven it has always played a part in it's defence. Following the scares of the Spanish Armada in 1588 Henry VIII had 2 defensive towers built, one, partly extant, on the eastern headland overlooking West Angle, the other, now vanished, on the opposite shore near St Ann's Head. Further 19th century fears, this time of French invasion, led to the establishment of an extensive system of defensible barracks and blockhouses. Often known as Palmerston's Follies, after a Prime Minister and Foreign Secretary of the time, there was a blockhouse, of which the gun emplacements remain, on the eastern headland, by Henry VIII's tower, and another on Thorn Island. Since the 1930s Thorn

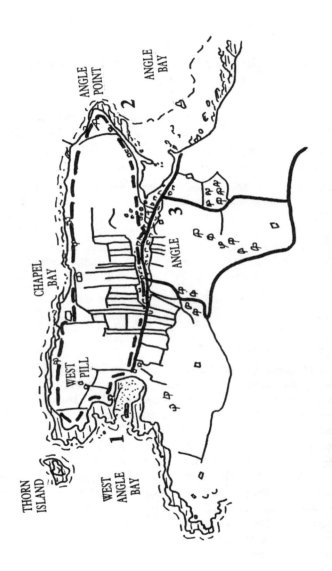

THORN ISLAND

WEST ANGLE BAY

1

WEST PILL

CHAPEL BAY

ANGLE

3

ANGLE POINT

2

ANGLE BAY

Island's grey eminence has found new uses as a summer hotel! There was another barracks at Chapel Bay, around the headland towards Angle Point, complete with an inland moat! During the 2nd World War Angle airfield was home to both spitfires and hurricanes. The masts from a disused RAF radio station are still visible on the horizon, above the old East Blockhouse.

Angle Brickworks flourished here from the 1870s, one of perhaps a dozen or so in the county. Producing bricks, tiles, and drain pipes, all that now remains is the brick chimney, behind the present café. To the right of the beach, just past the limekiln, is an old limestone quarry. Providing stone for Thorn Island, and lime for the brickworks and the land, there was at one time a tramway connecting quarry and brickworks, along the route taken by the present Coast Path. A passage blasted out on the seaward side has made it a sheltered harbour. There have always been wrecks around this dangerous coast; one of the most famous being the *Loch Shiel*, en route from Glasgow to Adelaide, Australia, with 7,000 cases of whiskey. Wrecked on Thorn Island in 1894 the crew were successfully rescued by the Angle lifeboat, but coincidentally only 2,000 of the whiskey cases were officially recovered! Angle people are a hardy race! One more recent disaster was the oil tanker *Sea Empress*, holed on the Mid Channel rocks at the entrance to the Haven in February 1996, leaking 70,000 tons of crude oil into the sea in the process. Whilst all visible traces of the oil spill have been virtually eradicated from the local beaches, there has, inevitably, been damage to the ecosystem — here at West Angle a rare colony of rockpool starfish has been virtually wiped out. There have been recent moves to declare the Pembrokeshire islands, the Milford Haven waterway and the Daugleddau river system north of the Cleddau Bridge a Special Area of Conservation, which may add some measure of protection, though this would no doubt create a few problems for the oil industry!

2. There has been a lifeboat at Angle since the 1860s. Originally known as the Milford Haven lifeboat the first station was built at Angle Point; the brick remains are all that are now left. The station moved permanently to it's present position in the 1920s. The

current station dates from 1992, the offshore lifeboat being *The Lady Rank*. So far some 330 lives have been saved. The area between Angle, and, across the water, the inlets of Dale and Sandy Haven, is traditionally the best area in the Haven for sea fishing, and Angle Bay has provided safe anchorage and shelter for countless fishermen and yachtsmen. The extensive mud flats provide important feeding grounds for wintering ducks and waders. The industrial minarets across the bay are those of Texaco refinery.

3. Angle's long main street, with it's flat roofed houses, colonnaded hotel and scattered medieval buildings, has a distinctiveness unique in Pembrokeshire. Taking it's name from it's geographical position, in an 'angle' of land, the village grew up around it's Norman landowners. Alongside the growing village were the strip fields which helped supply the Norman manor with food. These medieval strip fields are still there, and retain their original shape, stretched out as they are behind the houses on either side of the main street. The only difference now is that they are enclosed! Just north of the church is the 14th century sandstone tower house. Similar to tower houses in Ireland, Angle's tower house is unique in Wales. Above a vaulted undercroft are 3 storeys which would have been the living quarters. Access would have been at first floor level, thus allowing the occupants to seal themselves in should they be attacked. It was possibly the residence of the de Shirburn family, who were Lords of the Manor here from the late 13th to the 15th centuries. A short distance away, on private land, is a dovecote which would have provided plump pigeon pie for the table.

The church, dedicated to St Mary the Virgin, is 13th century, or at least the north wall and north transept are, the church was much restored in the 1850s. The tower is 15th century. There is a fishermen's chapel in the grounds. Dedicated to St Anthony it was built by Edward de Shirburn in 1447. There is also a tiered Preaching, or Calvary Cross, by the church entrance. Such crosses consist of a Latin cross mounted on 3 steps, symbolising Charity, Hope, and at the top, Faith. Just south of the main street, by the

Post Office, is another medieval building. Marked as a fortified dwelling on OS maps there has been speculation that it may have been a nunnery. Certainly pilgrims sailed from West Angle Bay to Ireland, and across the Haven, near Dale, is Monk Haven, where pilgrims landed en route to St David's. The distinctive flat roofed houses were built or restored at the end of the 19th century by the then owner of Angle estate to remind him of the building style he had encountered on a tour of duty in South Africa. Nowadays Angle is very much a residential village, with some second homes.

Walk Directions: [-] denotes Point of Interest

1. Starting from West Angle Bay [1] follow the track to West Pill Farm, shortly branching off to the left onto the Coast Path. Clearly signposted.

2. Continue on the Coast Path, passing opposite Thorn Island, and then past Chapel Bay and Angle lifeboat station to reach Angle Point [2]. This section of Coast Path provides the best view of the Haven and it's shipping.

3. From Angle Point continue on the track past the Point House pub. Where the track branches left over a bridge go straight ahead.

4. Just past the medieval tower house go through a gate and walk diagonally left to reach a play area. Go through the play area to reach the main road through Angle [3].

5. Turn right and continue to West Angle Bay and the starting point.

Facilities:

Parking also possible in Angle village, or in the car park for the Point House pub.

Most facilities available in Angle. BT telephone, public toilets, seasonal café and caravan park at West Angle Bay. Freshwater West, nearby, has one of the finest beaches and dune systems in the county, complete with renovated hut where edible seaweed was dried before being made into laver bread! Can be a dangerous beach for inexperienced swimmers.

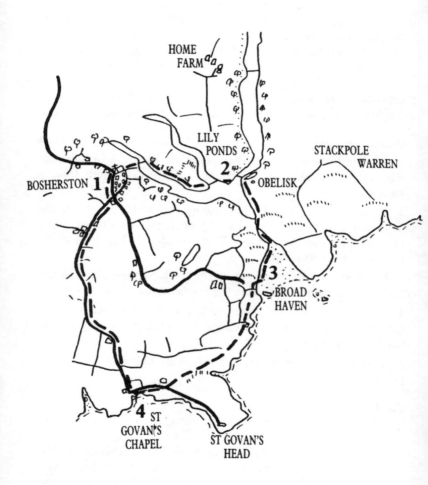

HOME
FARM

LILY
PONDS

2

OBELISK

STACKPOLE
WARREN

BOSHERSTON **1**

3

BROAD
HAVEN

4 ST
GOVAN'S
CHAPEL

ST GOVAN'S
HEAD

Bosherston - Lily Ponds - Broad Haven South - St Govan's Chapel - Bosherston

NB: Part of this walk is within Castlemartin Range. Check in Bosherston, or with Tourist Offices, Information Centres, or under Public Notices in the Western Telegraph, to see if firing is in progress.

OS Maps:	1:50 000 Tenby 158; 1:25 000 Outdoor Leisure 36 South Pembrokeshire/Castlemartin & St Govan's Head 1124 (SR 89/99)
Start:	Public footpath at Bosherston car park.
Access:	Bosherston is reached on the minor road from the B4319 Pembroke to Castlemartin road. Buses 364/365 and PostBus 395 operate from Pembroke Dock and Pembroke to Bosherston.
Parking:	Bosherston — car park next to St Michael's church.
Grade:	Easy — footpath, beach, field and grassland. Some road walking.

Points of Interest:

1. A pretty place to while away a summer's afternoon, with the Olde Worlde Café and lily ponds nearby. Bosherston, Bosher's Town, was given to Bosher, in the retinue of de Stackpole who came over with William the Conqueror. In the 13th century it was known as Stackpole Bosher, to distinguish it from nearby Stackpole Elidyr. The de Stackpoles more than likely took their name from the Norse for the area, 'stac' meaning a rock stack i.e. Church Rock and Star Rock guarding the entrance to Broad Haven, and 'pollr', a small inlet. The 11th century castle built by Elidur de Stackpole was superseded by a mansion, which in time was superseded by Stackpole Court, a Georgian mansion dating

from 1735. This in turn was demolished in the early 1960s. It's site is near the present Home Farm. By the late 17th century the estate, stretching from Freshwater West to Freshwater East, and north to Angle and Castlemartin, was in the hands of the Campbells of Cawdor, Scotland. In 1976 death duties led to the transfer of the estate to the nation, part of which is now administered by the National Trust.

The church of St Michael and All Angels is late 13th century, built on the site of an earlier church. It was restored in 1855 by the Cawdor family. The font is Norman. There is a Preaching, or Calvary Cross, in the grounds, set into a 2 tier stone base. It's probable date is 14th century. The head at the intersection is that of Christ, and may suggest that it was originaly a crucifix that had been mutilated during the Reformation, and, minus it's original stem, been converted to a Calvary Cross. The church gateway has what are known as 'Cock and Hen' gateposts, formerly common in the county at the entrances to farms and churches. The 2 gateposts are topped by stones of different sizes, the largest being the hen. They are believed to be Viking in origin — they had the friendly habit of displaying the heads of their enemies, male and female, on their stockades.

2. The lily ponds are an exhilarating area, particularly in May and June when they are at their best. A series of inter-connecting fish ponds comprising the western, middle and eastern arms they extend over some 80 acres and were created in the late 18th century/early 19th century by the Earl of Cawdor to enhance the Stackpole estate. The drowned river valley is protected from the sea by a shingle bank and sand bar, and as further guard against natural accidents, a man made retaining wall. The resultant freshwater pools provide good entertainment for coarse fishing; mostly pike, but there are plenty of perch, tench, eels and roach to try the temper. 3 delightful footbridges give access. Well frequented by herons, swans, coots, mallards, moorhens and the occasional kingfisher. Lady Margaret's Seat, giving a grand view over the area, is a late 19th century obelisk with 4 stone seats built

into it. There is a fine 3rd to 4th century BC Iron Age fort, known as Fishponds Camp, situated between the western and middle arms of the lily ponds. At that time the valley would have been open to the sea, and would have provided a good protected landing place for new settlers. The site is now overgrown with bramble and gorse and cannot be reached.

3. Broad Haven is frequently called Broad Haven South to distinguish it from Broad Haven on St Brides Bay. It is a fine sandy beach, backed by sand dunes, the youngest dunes those closest to the sea. The dune area of Stackpole Warren, as it's name implies, has been home to generations of rabbits, and it's warrens, both natural and artificial, were well used by rabbit catchers up until the 1950s. The warren is still fed by sand blown up from Broad Haven — all dunes require dry sand, with sufficient wind to drive it ashore. Once these conditions are right then marram grass can send out it's roots, and the accumulations of sand colonised and stabilised. Dunes offer the opportunity to view the progression from bare ground through to stable dunes, and on to thin turf and thicket. Plenty of plant life for exploration, the blues of viper's bugloss giving way to the red berries of sea buckthorn. The smaller of the 2 rocks guarding Broad Haven is Church Rock. It's profile, viewed from the car park area, bears an uncanny resemblance to King Kong! Good views from the sea's edge of the sheer cliffs of Stackpole Head and the softer outlines of Caldey Island.

4. St Govans chapel, built into the limestone cliffs at the only accessible point along this stretch of coast, has to be one of the best hermit's chapels in Britain. Despite legends connecting him with Sir Gawaine of Arthurian fame, St Govan is believed to be Gobhan or Gobban, the 6th century Abbot of Dairinis monastery in Wexford, Ireland. It is not known why he came to Pembrokeshire — perhaps there was a connection with St Ailbe, founder of Dairinis monastery, who originated from Solva, near St David's — whatever the reason he stayed the rest of his life in his cell in meditation and preaching. He died in 586. The present chapel dates from rebuilding in the 13th century (with a little recent help

from the National Park), though the walls and altar may date from the 6th century. Of interest is the doorway to the north of the altar, which gives access to a small chamber cut into the rock. Outside the chapel there is a rock boulder known as Bell Rock. Legend tells that St Govan was given a silver bell, which was stolen by pirates. St Govan, who as a saint was entitled to expect miracles, duly prayed for it's return, and accordingly it was retrieved by angels and placed inside the boulder for safekeeping. The rock, on being struck by St Govan, gave out a note a 1000 times louder than that of the original bell. To the south of the chapel there is a well, now dry, but which was visited until the 1850s for wishes and healing.

The Coastguard lookout on St Govan's Head is only used in rough weather. The limestone cliffs from Linney Head to Stackpole Head are amongst the finest in Britain, and provide fine climbing opportunities. Cliff caves, still extant, were well favoured by late Mesolithic, Neolithic and Bronze Age peoples, who have left behind bones of red deer, wolf, pig and fox, as well as pottery, flint and the odd human bone as evidence of their presence. It's not that they were great rock climbers, but that the lower sea levels and the freezing and thawing of the rock face resulted in cliff shattering and the formation of rubble slopes, often reaching from the foot of the slope to the top. It makes for easier access! Castlemartin peninsula came to the attention of the War Department in 1939, and the old storage magazines and some of the rails from that time are visible in the St Govan's Head area. After 57 years as a Royal Armoured Corps range Castlemartin Range is now a field training centre for the Army. There are rare guided walks along the coast through the range from Stack Rocks to Freshwater West, but given the extraordinary beauty and importance of the limestone cliffs this level of access is unacceptable.

Walk Directions: [-] denotes Point of Interest

1. Start from the car park in Bosherston **[1]** — the car park is next to the church. Cross the car park and take the path leading downhill to the lily ponds.

2. At the 1st lily pond take the path bearing left. There is a footpath sign here, marked 'Pumphouse'. The left arm indicates Broad Haven is 1 mile away. Follow the path and cross the 1st footbridge.

3. Continue on the path leading around the pond to cross a 2nd footbridge. The path from here ascends to meet a track. Bear right; the junction is marked by the footpath sign 'Middle Arm' [2].

4. The path descends to a 3rd footbridge, marked by another footpath sign — 'Grassy Bridge'. Turn right and cross the bridge. Continue on the sandy path, keeping to the pond edge, to reach the junction of the lily ponds and Broad Haven. Again another footpath sign — marked 'Outlet'.

5. Cross the wooden footbridge to gain Broad Haven beach [3]. Keeping the outlet stream to your left cross the beach in front of the sand dunes to gain Broad Haven car park. The way up from the beach to the car park is marked by wooden railings and has some stone steps to help in the short ascent.

6. Turn left at the top of the path and cross the car park to a wooden stile leading into a field. Signpost at the stile indicates 'Coast Path'.

7. Cross the field to Castlemartin Range entrance stile and gate. There is a range hut, with warning notices clearly displayed. If there are red flags flying do not cross! Assuming all is well cross the range. The path route is marked by white posts — and there are plenty of signs marked 'Danger — Military Firing Range — Keep Out' to keep you on the path. A safe stroll through the gorse, with (in winter at least) plenty of sheep for company!

8. Where the range path joins the tarmac road leading to the Coastguard lookout there is the option to detour left to the lookout, or continue right, crossing by a cattle grid, to St Govan's chapel [4] and the car park.

9. The route down to St Govan's chapel is indicated by a 6 pointed star. Some 74 steps will lead you down — though legend has it that it is impossible to count the same number of steps going back up as were counted on the way down!

10. Return to Bosherston and the starting point along the tarmac

road leading inland away from the chapel and car park. The road passes Royal Navy Control Tower Newton, and a smaller range hut 'Newton', both on the left hand side.

Facilities:

Parking also possible at Broad Haven (seasonal charge), and at St Govan's chapel.

Pub, Post Office, public toilets, and BT telephone in Bosherston. Also a seasonal café — Ye Olde Worlde Café, and a Coastguard station (occasionally manned). Public toilets at Broad Haven car park. Emergency telephones at St Govan's Head (Coastguard lookout) and St Govan's chapel range entrance. Coarse fishing permits are available from Ye Olde Worlde Café and National Trust office at Stackpole. Barafundle Bay, one of the finest beaches in Pembrokeshire, is reached only on the Coast Path, either from Broad Haven and Stackpole Head, or from Stackpole Quay — well worth the visit; stunning cliff scenery en route! Easily extended to create a circular walk by continuing to Stackpole Quay and Stackpole village, returning to Bosherston via Stackpole estate and the eastern arm of the lily ponds. Pub in Stackpole village, seasonal tea rooms at Stackpole Quay.

Manorbier - Presipe - King's Quoit
- Manorbier Bay - Swanlake Bay - East Moor
- Manorbier

2 for the price of 1 — this walk can be split into 2 walks of 3 miles/4.75 kilometres each if preferred!

OS Maps:	1:50 000 Tenby 158; 1:25 000 Outdoor Leisure 36 South Pembrokeshire/Manorbier & Tenby 1125 (SS 09/19)
Start:	National Park car park.
Access:	Manorbier is reached from the A4139 Pembroke to Tenby road, and is equidistant between the 2 towns. Buses 358/359 Tenby — Pembroke — Haverfordwest stop at Manorbier. Manorbier train station (service Swansea — Tenby — Pembroke Dock) is just over a mile/1.5 kilometres north of the village.
Parking:	Either free parking in front of 'The Dak', or in the National Park car park below Manorbier Castle — seasonal charge.
Grade:	Moderate. Coastal path, field, green lane and road — there is a fairly steep section at East Moor Cliff.

Points of Interest:

1. The origin of Manorbier as a place name is uncertain. One interpretation has it as the Maenor Pyrr, that is a holding of land by Pyrrus or Pir, the 6th century first Abbot of Caldey Island monastery. It is known that Caldey had farming estates on the mainland. Not much is known of Pyrrus, though it is known that after a night of too much local wine he drowned in the abbey

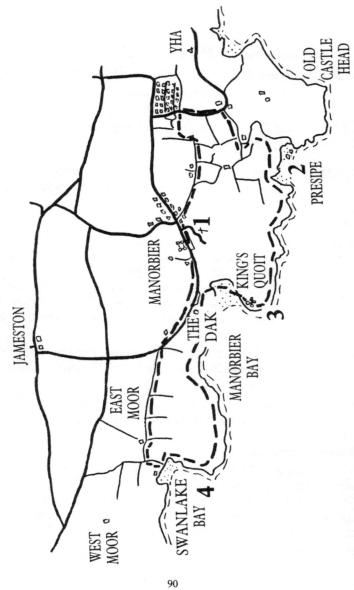

fishpond! The present spelling dates from the 1860s. The Norman history of Manorbier began when Odo de Barri was given lands here as a reward for military service, sometime shortly after the Norman invasion of Pembrokeshire in 1093. His son William began the building of the stone castle in the 12th century, though most of it's construction dates from between 1230 to 1260. More of a fortified mansion than a fortress new farming techniques were introduced which added new types of food, and a surplus for sale at that, to the oats, barley, meat and dairy produce normally consumed.

To the Norman colony were brought Flemish builders, farmers and tradesmen to supplant the local Welsh. An open field system was introduced, with water mill for grinding corn, fishpond, orchard, deerpark and dovecote added. The dovecote still stands, reached on the footpath/road below the castle (located nearly opposite the National Park car park entrance). It is just past the ruins of a second, later mill. The original mill and fishpond were situated in the valley between the castle and the church. Manorbier Castle was fortunate never to be attacked, partly due to the Welsh connections of the de Barris, partly because it was out of the way of the more imposing fortress castles. Nearly a ruin by the 19th century it was rescued in the 1880s by the talented renovations of J.R. Cobb.

The church across the valley is originally Norman, it's imposing tower dating from 1270. Dedicated to St James the Great it was restored from 1867 to 1870. Worth a visit for it's unusual interior. Like many early ecclesiastical buildings it has a circular graveyard. Like it's near neighbours Tenby and Saundersfoot it's popularity as a seaside resort began from the mid 18th century and the building of the Pembroke to Tenby Railway in 1863. Manorbier came to be seen as little more exclusive than Tenby. In the centre of the village, opposite the Post Office, is the restored Bier House, nothing to do with the local pubs, the history of the village or the origin of it's name, but built in 1900 to house the parish bier!

Of Gerald of Wales and Welsh Hospitality

Manorbier's most famous son was born Gerald de Barri, son of William de Barri and Angharad de Carew, granddaughter of the last Prince of South Wales, Rhys ap Tewdwr, in circa 1146. Scholar, intellectual, politician and ecclesiastic, he was made Archdeacon of Brecon at 28, lectured in law at the University of Paris, and was chaplain and tutor to the young Richard I and King John.

He spent much of his life campaigning to become Bishop of St David's and struggling with Henry II to create a Welsh National Church. His failure to do so was probably due to him being too Welsh and too capable for Henry's uses. If this was not enough he still found time to pen 17 books, of which the 'Description of Wales' and 'Journey through Wales', and the 'History and Topography of Ireland', are the best known, and which are still in print! His life earned him the title of Gerald of Wales, or Giraldus Cambrensis. He died in 1223, at the ripe old age of 77.

In his books he writes lively and entertaining prose, extolling the virtues of the Welsh, and his homeland of Wales and Manorbier. Here he is, in his 'Description of Wales' from circa 1191, on the virtues of the Welsh, in this case their hospitality and generosity. 'When you travel there is no question of your asking for accommodation or of their offering it: you just march into a house and hand over your weapons to the person in charge. They give you water so that you may wash your feet and that means you are a guest . . . Guests who arrive early in the day are entertained until nightfall by girls who play to them on the harp . . . '

Go for it!

★ ★ ★

2. Presipe has a fine, sandy beach, with no access to it by car. The many stacks and rocks make it an interesting area for rockpool explorers, with plenty of sea anemones, crabs, starfish and those chameleons of the rockpool fish world, the blenny. The Atlantic

gales and tides which hammer this southern coast can leave unusual visitors. I have seen jellyfish stranded by the tide, decked out in fine white, purple and yellow, with a thin, neat black line for a border, and tentacles splayed out on one side like silver chains. Old Castle Head, above, was once an Iron Age fort. During World War I airships, acting in accord with the hydrophone station on Carn Llidi on St David's Head, used to leave for photographic reconnaissance, on constant lookout for submarines. The site is now a Royal Artillery Range. Good views south to Lundy Island on a clear day.

3. King's Quoit is a Neolithic cromlech, or burial chamber, dating from circa 3,000 B.C. Unusual, in that the main distribution of the cromlechs are on the northern coast, use may well have been made of a loose ledge from the ridge above to act as a capstone. However 1 of the 3 supporting pillars has fallen. There is no record of any skeleton being found. There have been both Mesolithic and Neolithic flint finds at Manorbier and around the headland at Swanlake Bay — the tides then would have been further out, away from the present shoreline, and at exceptionally low tides there are the remains of a prehistoric forest.

4. Swanlake Bay, like Presipe, is another isolated beach, accessible only from the Coast Path, or on footpaths from East and West Moor farms. It's sandy beach and isolation make it a popular alternative to the more crowded beaches of Freshwater East or Manorbier. Both East Moor and West Moor farms were original Norman land grant farms, under the lordship of Manorbier.

Walk Directions: [-] denotes Point of Interest

1. From the National Park car park turn right onto the road and walk uphill towards Manorbier [1]. Ignore the first turning right to St James' church, instead continue and turn right by the Castlemead Hotel.

2. Follow the road past the houses onto a farm lane. Ignore the turning right and continue left to reach a stile giving access to a green lane — there is a good limekiln on the left just past the stile.

3. Continue straight ahead on the green lane to meet a short path bearing left uphill into a field.

4. Follow the path around to the right and cross the field to a road — there is a children's play area on the left here.

5. Turn right onto the road and continue uphill to turn right across a stile just before the boundary of Manorbier Royal Artillery Range — the road itself continues around left to Skrinkle Haven and the youth hostel. You are now on the Coast Path.

6. Follow the yellow waymarkers adjacent to the boundary fence, to cross 2 fields, and then turn left over a stile into a 3rd field.

7. Go straight ahead, bearing slightly left, to reach the stile giving access to the cliff path.

8. Continue on the Coast Path, passing Presipe on your left [2] — steep steps will lead you down to the beach — and follow the Path for a mile/1.5 kilometres around to King's Quoit [3] and Manorbier Bay.

9. Cross Manorbier beach to cross a stream by a stone footbridge and climb the steps cut into the rock to gain the path passing in front of a parking bay.

10. Follow the path through 'The Dak' grounds and continue on the Coast Path for well over a mile/1.5 kilometres to Swanlake Bay [4].

11. Cross the stile at the head of the beach and immediately turn right and follow the steep steps uphill to a field.

12. Keep to the right field edge, until just before a farm gate, cross a stone stile into another field.

13. Keep to the left field edge to meet a wooden stile into the farm lane at East Moor. Turn right, then shortly left to cross another stone stile.

14. Cross 3 fields, keeping to the left edge, to meet the minor road leading to Manorbier.

15. Turn right onto the road and follow it down to Manorbier and the starting point.

Facilities:

Parking also possible in Manorbier itself, or in the parking bay by 'The Dak'.

Manorbier offers a Post Office, BT telephone, shops, café and pub. Public toilets by the castle entrance, and at the National Park car park. Emergency phone at National Park car park toilets. Manorbier Castle and garden open daily Easter to September 30. Picnic site and youth hostel at Skrinkle Haven.

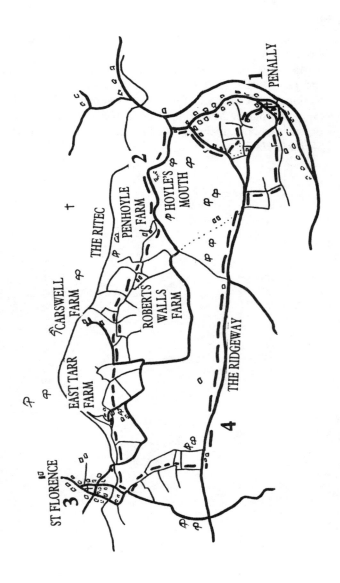

PENALLY 1

HOYLE'S MOUTH

PENHOYLE FARM 2

THE RITEC

CARSWELL FARM

EAST TARR FARM

ROBERTS WALLS FARM

ST FLORENCE 3

THE RIDGEWAY 4

Penally - Hoyle's Mouth - St Florence - The Ridgeway - Penally

OS Maps:	1:50 000 Tenby 158; 1:25 000 Outdoor Leisure 36 South Pembrokeshire/Tenby & Manorbier 1125 (SS 09/19)
Start:	Penally church.
Access:	Penally is situated on the A4139, just south west of Tenby. Buses 358/359 from Tenby to Pembroke and Haverfordwest stop at Penally, as does the train from Swansea and Tenby to Pembroke Dock. Bus 360 from Tenby to Carew stops at St Florence.
Parking:	Parking by Penally church.
Grade:	Moderate — mainly field paths with some road walking.

Points of Interest:

1. Penally is clustered around it's smart hill, a fitting backdrop to the glorious sweep of Tenby's south beach. The present name is a corruption of Penalun, head of the river Alun, now culverted. St Teilo, an influential 6th century contemporary of St David, was reputedly born here. There was a monastery in the area at one time, but the site is now lost. The ruins in the grounds of Penally Abbey Hotel may be those of a chapel dedicated to St Deiniol, with whom the well, strikingly set in the lane wall opposite, is associated. The well may be a survival of a pre-Christian past, for wells, rivers and sacred trees were objects of devotion in Celtic religion. They would have had their own particular god, and their cult would be maintained by local druids, who would arrange for any particular public or private sacrifices! The Norman church, in it's splendid setting amongst the palms, is 13th century, with a 14th century porch and probable 16th century tower. It is dedicated to St

Nicholas of Myra, patron saint of seafarers. There is, in the south transept, a fine and rare sandstone tomb, with, on either side of a worn Calvary Cross, the heads of a man and woman. The inscription, in Norman French, is tQ William and Isamay de Naunton.

There are three 9th and 10th century crosses in the church which would originally have stood outside in the present churchyard. They may have been carved for the monastery. The broken shafts of 2 are now all that remain, the 3rd is complete and has a fine, delicate wheel headed cross. Of the 2 now on display the complete stone has Celtic knotwork culminating, in the front, in a vine scroll; the other shows what appear to be reptiles devouring each other. These Celtic crosses provide evidence of the early history of Christianity, set up to commemorate individuals many have survived, whereas the early religious cells have long since vanished or been built over. Penally's crosses are lighter in touch, and more finely lyrical in spirit than the 2 other major Pembrokeshire Celtic crosses at Carew and Nevern, which are heavier and more powerful in expression. Penally is now a flourishing and modern village, after all the first house in Pembrokeshire to install electricity was here! It has grown much in size and popularity over the last half a century or so.

2. Hoyle's Mouth is a natural limestone cave cut out by the action of water. Like other limestone caves here on Longbury Bank, at Cat's Hole near Monkton, and on Caldey Island (then a hill on the Carmarthen plain), they provided shelter for families and clans of Stone Age peoples moving north from Europe. Arriving by 20,000 BC, before the onset of the last great ice sheet, they may have been forced to retreat before the shifting ice, to return again from 15,000 BC onwards. Living at, or near, the cave entrance, these hunter gatherers, like Jean Auel's 'Clan of the Cave Bear', shared territory with cave lions, cave bears, hyenas, hippos and rhinoceros. Looking out from their fire warm caves they would have seen tundra and steppe land stretching out across the great plain of the Bristol Channel to beyond present day Ireland, with southern Britain still connected to Europe. Across the great plain roamed

reindeer, elk and mammoth which provided a great source of food and clothes. Finds here at Hoyle's Mouth, and at other caves close by, include reindeer and horse, cave bear, woolly mammoth and hyena, as well as simple tools.

By 10,000 BC the last of the ice from the Irish Sea glacier had melted, Milford Haven's river valley was a flood, and by circa 7,000 BC Britain was an island. With the drowning of the coastal areas Pembrokeshire began to assume it's present shape. The river Ritec, below, was a tidal river, and during the Middle Ages ships and barges made their way 3 miles/5 kilometres upriver to St Florence. From 1811 to 1820 an embankment was built across it's mouth to create new pasture land. The 1863 Pembroke to Tenby Railway was laid across the top of this embankment. The result is extensive reedbeds and marshland. Tenby Marsh and the surrounding area are home to the Tenby daffodil; unique to the area it has a fine golden yellow sheen and a trumpet longer than the surrounding petals.

3. Prior to the arrival of the Normans St Florence may have been known as Tregoyr, but seems to have acquired the name St Florence when the church, begun in the 12th century, was dedicated to St Florentius, a popular 5th century Norman saint. A medieval woollen centre in the 12th century, St Florence had access to the sea on a high tide, no doubt an asset to trade. There are the ruins of an old corn mill, known as Causey Mill, alongside the Ritec. Documentary map evidence dates it to the 14th century, but it may well be older. Mills like this were part and parcel of the fabric of rural life, and local grown grain went to produce flour for bread and animal feed. However the miller's tale soon became a lament when in the 19th century cheap grain imports ended a centuries old way of life. There is a splendid 1861 engraving of the mill reproduced on an information board inside the mill. Note the thatched roof! The area is noted for some splendid chimneys, known locally as Flemish chimneys, which have been built onto the outside of 16th and 17th century houses — there is another fine round chimney at Corn Mwg in Penally. There is little evidence to

connect them with the Flemish, perhaps they were seen as incomers the way the Flemings were seen who came to settle and work in the woollen trade under the Norman occupation, Flemish meaning foreign. St Florence is one of the best and most attractive of the Norman villages south of the Landsker, clustered as it is around it's church. A constant winner of village in bloom awards!

4. The Ridgeway is a long ridge of Old Red Sandstone stretching from Lamphey in the west to Tenby. Like the Flemings Way across the Preselis to the north the Ridgeway would have been used as a trackway by Neolithic and Bronze Age peoples travelling to Pembroke and the Castlemartin peninsula. One indicator of Bronze Age settlement are the round barrows frequently sited on high ground and on trackways so that they can be easily seen. Carew and Norchard Beacons, both to the west of St Florence, had tumuli. From Norchard Beacon the inner reaches of the Cleddau are visible, with the Norman Benton and Carew castles in sight, as well as Carmarthen Bay to the south. The great limestone head of Lydstep Point is visible, below south, curling around to shelter it's magnificent bay.

Caldey Island, 'cold island' as the Norse called it, was originally Ynys Pyr, the island of Pyr, the abbot of the first religious house in the early 6th century. Most of the present abbey and church were built by the Benedictines from 1910 to 1912. The island was sold off in 1926, and is now home to the Cistercians, former holders of Tintern and Fountains abbeys. One relatively recent visitor to the island was the Emperor Haile Selassie of Ethiopia, who found a brief refuge there during the 2nd World War. St Margaret's Island, close by, is the largest cormorant colony in England and Wales, with usually 250 pairs a year — though numbers have dropped since the tanker *Sea Empress* spilled 70,000 tons of crude oil in February 1996. The ruined buildings are old quarrymen's cottages.

Tenby, with it's 13th century castle and town walls, has to be one of the most favoured spots in Wales. An important fishing and trading centre in Tudor and Stuart times Tenby's later fortunes, and elegance, as a holiday resort owe much to the efforts of Sir William Paxton in the early 19th century. Tenby's south beach was the favoured landing place of the 'peregrini', early saints and pilgrims who would have landed here, en route to St David's, Whitesand Bay and Ireland. The beach is backed by the Burrows, a dune system as fine as Freshwater West's, and the oldest golf course in Wales. Given clear weather good views south of Lundy Island and the coast of Devon.

Walk Directions: [-] denotes Point of Interest

1. Starting from the church in Penally [1] walk up the lane to the left of Penally Abbey Hotel — sign here marked 'Penally Nature Trail'. After a short distance St Deiniol's Well is passed on the left.

2. At the entrance to Penally Manor leave the lane through an iron gate on the right (or cross the stile), and ascend on a woodland path, crossing a stone stile en route, to enter a field over a wooden stile. Great views of Tenby and Carmarthen Bay now open up.

3. Keeping to the left field edge continue into a 2nd field. Cross diagonally right the 2nd field to reach an iron gate. Go through the gate and descend on a grassy and steep track to reach the tarmac road by Frankleston House.

4. Turn right and follow the road to the T junction opposite the Paddock Inn. Turn left and continue to shortly turn left again — sign here marked 'Ritec Valley Buggies 1 mile'.

5. Continue on the road, passing Trefloyne golf course on the left. A short way past the golf course, on the left above, is Hoyle's Mouth cave [2]. There is a path leading up to the cave entrance through a stone gateway. The path leads off opposite a telegraph pole and farm gate — the telegraph pole is marked with a yellow arrow.

6. Continue past Penhoyle Fishing Park to reach Penhoyle Farm. To the left of the entrance is a public footpath, signposted. Go ahead on the path, initially wooded, to reach a field. Cross the field, keeping to the right field edge.

7. Cross 2 stiles to enter another field — here there is a diversion to the footpath marked on the OS maps. Cross diagonally right to reach a stile just to the right of Roberts Walls Farm, home to the Ritec Valley buggies — all terrain vehicles for cross country driving. Cross the stile, and keeping to the left field edge, cross 2 fields to reach a stile giving access to scrubland.

8. Continue ahead, enter another field over a stile, and then shortly turn to the right over another stile and turn left to meet the lane to Ashdene and Carswell Farm.

9. Turn left and follow the lane to reach a stone stile just where the lane turns sharp left. Cross 2 fields to reach the road to East Tarr Farm. Turn right and then left onto a green lane, signposted just past the first building on the left.

10. Continue on the green lane to cross 2 wooden stiles into a field. Keeping to the right edge cross the field to meet a woodland path. Follow the path until it meets the minor road to St Florence.

11. Turn right, and then left just before the old mill, and follow the path alongside the river Ritec to reach the clapper bridge and ford on the road into St Florence. Well worth taking time out to divert here and explore St Florence [3].

12. From the clapper bridge and ford follow the road to a T junction. Turn left and almost immediately cross a stile into a field. Keeping to the left edge shortly cross a stile left, and then keeping to the right edge continue uphill over 4 more stiles to reach the Ridgeway [4].

13. Turn left, and continue for just over 1.5 miles/2.5 kilometres to reach 2 stiles on either side of the road. Cross right and head left across the field to a stile at the bottom left of field. Cross a 2nd field, keeping to the left edge, to reach another stile at the bottom left.

14. Cross onto a green lane, and continue, past residential houses, to reach Strawberry Lane. Turn right and continue downhill. Turn left onto the road passing in front of the Cross Inn, and continue back to the church and the starting point.

Facilities:

Parking also possible in St Florence and on the Ridgeway.

All facilities available in Penally, most in St Florence. Roberts Walls Farm offers Ritec Valley buggies, and there is Manor House Wildlife and Leisure Park just outside St Florence, as are a Country Sports Park and a Dinosaur Park! Penhoyle Fishing Park and Community Woodlands, by Hoyle's Mouth, is open to the public.

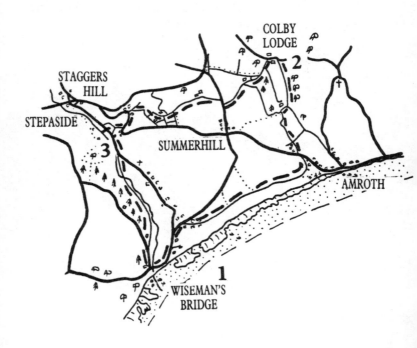

STAGGERS HILL

COLBY LODGE

STEPASIDE

2

SUMMERHILL

AMROTH

3

1

WISEMAN'S BRIDGE

Wiseman's Bridge - Amroth - Colby Lodge
- Summerhill - Staggers Hill - Pleasant Valley
- Wiseman's Bridge

Can be combined with Walk 14 to make a single walk of 7 miles/11 kilometres by omitting the Amroth to Colby Lodge section.

OS Maps:	1:50 000 Tenby 158; 1:25 000 Outdoor Leisure 36 South Pembrokeshire/Tenby & Saundersfoot 1104 (SN 00/10).
Start:	Wiseman's Bridge.
Access:	Wiseman's Bridge is on the coastal road between Saundersfoot and Amroth. It is 1 mile/1.5 kilometres south of Stepaside. Buses 350 (Kilgetty-Amroth-Tenby) and 351 (Pendine-Amroth-Tenby) stop at Wiseman's Bridge. Nearest train stations Saundersfoot and Kilgetty.
Parking:	Wiseman's Bridge sea front.
Grade:	Moderate — coastal path, field, green lane, road.

Points of Interest:

1. Wiseman's Bridge takes it's name from one Andrew Wiseman who held half a knight's fee here; no Wiseman from the East this, but a Norman coloniser who reputedly accompanied an Earl of Pembroke, Aymer de Valence, from Normandy to Pembrokeshire in the early 14th century. There is a fine pebble banked storm beach, with at low tide a superb expanse of golden sand stretching

some 3 miles/5 kilometres from Amroth to Saundersfoot. A full scale mock landing for D Day took place here in 1943, with landing craft, barges, guns and soldiers scattered along the sea-lashed beach from Pendine to Saundersfoot. Eisenhower, Churchill and Montgomery were on site to supervise, Churchill being properly entertained by the Wiseman's Bridge Inn! An earlier army found a similar use, when in 1153 the sands and cliffs echoed to the march of a royal army of the sons of the Prince of West Wales, en route to surprise and destroy the Norman garrison at Tenby. The present Coast Path along the cliff top was once the main county road from Saundersfoot to Amroth, but the collapse of iron ore workings in the cliffs below made the road impracticable.

Geologically the area forms part of the South Wales Coalfield, and the belt of coal running across Pembrokeshire from Saundersfoot to Landshipping, Hook and Nolton has come to be termed the Daugleddau Coalfield. Records show coal mining dating back to at least the 14th century, with coal forming the major county export by 1700. However there was no attempt to exploit the potential of the local anthracite — amongst the finest in the world, and much favoured by Queen Victoria for it's smokeless quality — until the 19th century. In 1829 the Saundersfoot Railway and Harbour Company was authorised, and by 1832 the harbour and one main line inland were in operation. Prior to the harbour's opening cargoes were loaded directly onto ships from the beach at Saundersfoot and Wiseman's Bridge. In 1842 the line was extended through 3 tunnels and along the cliff edge to Wiseman's Bridge, turning inland along Pleasant Valley to the Stepaside and Kilgetty collieries. Coal was hauled in drams by horse and oxen, until, in 1874, the line was relaid and the locomotive *Rosalind* brought into service. The fortunes of the local collieries fluctuated, some closed, only to re-open, but by 1939 the coal industry here had ceased operations, and after 1945 the line was dismantled. Tourism was now the major industry. The last Pembrokeshire colliery to close was at Hook, inland on the river Cleddau, in 1949. The old railway line along the coast from Saundersfoot is now part of the Coast Path. From Wiseman's Bridge it is a short 1 mile/1.75

kilometre walk into Saundersfoot, the tunnels cool and pleasant on warm summer days!

2. Colby Lodge was built for the industrialist John Colby in 1803 to a Nash design. The natural woodland here is believed to be a remnant of the great medieval forest of Coedrath which extended from Saundersfoot to Amroth. The timber would have been a useful source of fuel, the poor only using coal when they could not afford wood. However with timber running short by the 1600s use would have been made of the local anthracite, and both coal and iron ore were extensively mined on the Colby estate during the 19th century. Nowadays little remains of the area's natural resources! Transport of coal from inland collieries to Saundersfoot harbour during their heyday in the 19th and early 20th centuries was, away from the railway lines, by carts, many pulled by teams of oxen and horses. As a result many roads were deeply rutted and often impassable. Turnpike Trusts were set up to improve conditions, but prices were so high that the local populace was alienated. Toll gates were smashed by Rebecca rioters, that at nearby Killanow crossroads being no exception. The Killanow notice board, giving prices for animals, carts and men, has survived and has found it's way to Colby Lodge's café. What price oxen and donkeys these days!

3. Whilst coal was the mainstay of local industry — there were 2 important collieries at Stepaside — the Pembrokeshire Coal and Iron Company opened an ironworks in 1849 on the site of the present Caravan Park. Most of the iron ore was dug out of the cliffs between Saundersfoot and Amroth by teams of 2 men, each team working some 50 'patches'. To provide fuel for the new ironworks a further colliery, Grove, was opened on the hills above in 1856. Stepaside Ironworks built up a reputation for quality, and became the terminus for the railway line from Saundersfoot, but by 1877 foreign competition proved too much and the ironworks closed. Grove Colliery had already closed in 1873. Many of the buildings of both Grove and the ironworks have survived, though in a ruined state — most impressive is the casting house, which now houses an

open air swimming pool! There have been plans to turn the area into a heritage park, with a narrow gauge railway running from Stepaside along Pleasant Valley to Wiseman's Bridge, however no ice cream express as yet!

Walk Directions: [-] denotes Point of Interest

1. Starting from Wiseman's Bridge **[1]** walk past the Wiseman's Bridge Inn and continue uphill, past the turning left to Pleasant Valley and Stepaside, to turn right onto a 'No Through Road'. Signposted 'Coast Path'. (Alternatively, if the tide is low, walk along the beach to Amroth!)

2. At the end of the road join the coastal path. Continue, passing a caravan park on the left — good views right of Carmarthen Bay and, at low tide, the wide sandy beach below.

3. After just over 0.5 miles/0.75 kilometres the Coast Path continues right over a stile. Continue instead ahead on the Public Path to cross a stile by a gate onto a green lane.

4. Continue to the Amroth road. Turn left, cross the road, and shortly turn right onto a Public Path passing in front of houses. Continue past the houses to reach a grassy path by a stile. Good views of Colby Lodge ahead, in the trees.

5. Cross 2 fields, keeping to the left edge, to meet a T junction. Turn right (the direction not signposted!) — and continue down alongside a stream, cross an old stone footbridge, and walk up to the path leading to Colby Lodge. Turn left.

6. At Colby Lodge **[2]** turn left onto the minor road, continue past the lodge, and shortly turn left onto a bridleway. Cross the stream by an attractive stone footbridge and go uphill, ignoring the stile and footpath on the right, to emerge onto a lane leading to the house on the right.

7. Follow the lane to the main road — Summerhill is immediately left. Turn right, cross the road, and take the left turn to Cwmrath Farm. Footpath sign here of a walking man.

8. Continue to the farm. Just before the farm buildings turn left

and drop down onto a path — there is a Public Footpath sign at foot height on the left. Continue on a wooded green lane.

9. Where the green lane meets a well defined farm lane turn right. After a short distance the footpath continues left by a farm gate to meet a stile giving access to a field. Cross the stile, turn right, and keeping to the right field edge continue to reach another stile.

10. Cross the stile, and head diagonally left downhill to another stile giving access to the road at Staggers Hill — if in doubt of which path to follow aim for the houses at Staggers Hill below!

11. Once at Staggers Hill turn left onto the tarmac road and continue uphill. After a short distance there is a signposted path, right, leading down steps into a field.

12. Follow the path alongside the field edge to reach a stile on the left giving access to Mill House Caravan Park. Continue across the park to the road. To the right is Stepaside. Turn left.

13. Almost immediately, opposite Mill House, there is a path on the right hand side, signposted with a metal walking man. Go ahead on this path — there is another caravan park on the right, once the site of Stepaside Ironworks [3].

14. Continue on the path — this was once the railway track carrying coal down to Saundersfoot harbour. There are still 1 or 2 stone sleepers left on the track. Continue through Pleasant Valley to Wiseman's Bridge and the starting point.

Facilities:

Parking also possible at Colby Lodge, Summerhill, or in the Stepaside area.

B&B, caravan parks and camping at Wiseman's Bridge — seasonal toilets (closed November to March), BT telephone and pub. Colby Lodge woodland gardens and café open April to beginning of November, gallery open year round. Bird and animal park, and craft village at Stepaside, as well as pub and caravan parks. Summerhill has a shop and BT telephone.

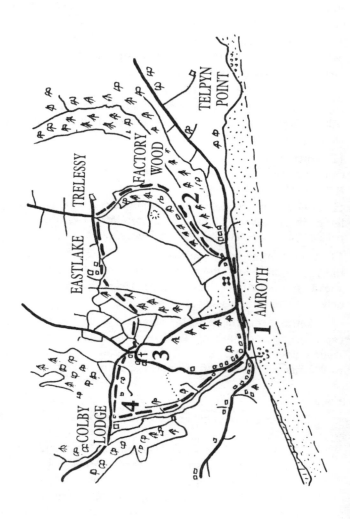

Amroth - Factory Wood - Eastlake
- Amroth Church - Colby Lodge - Amroth

May be combined with Walk 13 to create a walk of 7 miles/11 kilometres by omitting the Colby Lodge to Amroth section.

OS Maps:	1:50 000 Tenby 158; 1:25 000 Outdoor Leisure 36 South Pembrokeshire/Tenby & Saundersfoot 1104 (SN 00/10).
Start:	Amroth sea front — approximately halfway between Amroth Castle and the New Inn.
Access:	Amroth is situated on the coast road between Saundersfoot, Wiseman's Bridge, and Pendine in Carmarthenshire. Bus services 350 (Kilgetty — Amroth — Tenby) and 351 (Pendine — Amroth — Tenby).
Parking:	Anywhere along Amroth seafront — there is also a free National Park car park opposite the Amroth Arms, on the road leading to Amroth church.
Grade:	Easy — woodland paths, field and farm track, a little road walking.

Points of Interest:

1. The name Amroth ('Am-rath') may mean on, or near, the river Rath (believed to have been the name of 1 of the parish's boundary streams), or on, or near, the fort, and in various spellings can be traced back to at least 1220. Amroth's history as a village, however, dates back only as far as the mid 19th century. Prior to this a traveller journeying along the coast would have found only a scattering of houses near the church or the gentry mansions. However Amroth was on the edge of the Daugleddau Coalfield,

itself a continuation of the South Wales Coalfield, and with 19th century industrial expansion both coal and iron ore were in demand. Between Amroth and Saundersfoot there were some 50 'patches', each worked by 2 men who dug for iron ore in the cliffs. To the north of the village there developed the coal mining collieries of Coombes and Castlepark, small brothers of the larger Bonville's Court Colliery near Saundersfoot, and the Stepaside collieries. Amroth developed into a miners' village, close by the cliffs that gave many work.

The sea has always been jealous of the land here. Some 7,000 years ago there was a forest stretching far out from the present shoreline, the petrified remains still visible at exceptionally low tides. More recently, in the 1930s, the village at it's western end had houses on both sides of the road, but the storms soon put paid to their bright optimism, and they had to be demolished as unsafe. The present system of groynes along the beach are a modern attempt to further deny the sea. The great stretch of sand around to Wiseman's Bridge played host to mock landings in preparation for the Normandy landings during the Second World War. Nowadays the invasions occur during summer, and are much more peaceful in purpose! On clear days good views of Caldey Island, Tenby and Saundersfoot on the right, with the Gower peninsula and the Worm's Head framing Carmarthen Bay to the left.

The castle is recent, dating from the early 19th century, though it is on, or near the site of the Norman Eareweare Castle, all traces of which have now vanished. The Norman castle was dealt a fatal blow by Prince Llywelyn, who in the early 1200s was in the process of reclaiming, albeit temporarily, much of South West Wales from the alien Norman colonisers. Rebuilt at various times, and in various forms, the present castle has been converted to holiday flats, with caravans and chalets in the grounds. One early 19th century resident and local worthy rejoiced in the delightful title of the Reverend Thomas Shrapnel Biddulph. One wonders if his sermons were as explosive as his name!

2. Factory Wood no doubt owes it's name to the house halfway along the wooded track up to Trelessy. Known as 'The Factory' it is believed that clogs were made here to clothe 19th century feet. Alder was used for the sole, and there are still alder trees in Factory Wood, and nearby Little Trelissey Wood. It is believed the leather for the uppers was tanned nearby, close to Telypn Point, just over the boundary in Carmarthenshire. In a private field to the west of Factory Wood there is a settlement, marked 'Roman Building' on the OS 1:25 000 green covered Pathfinder map. The Roman military occupation took little notice of Pembrokeshire — perhaps the local Demetae were seen as too peaceable to require conquest — and Carmarthen remained their most westerly fort. However there is evidence of trade in finds of pottery and coins, and there are sites of Roman character. The circular earthwork here at Trelessy has been found to have contained a rectangular stone building, in occupation during the 2nd and 3rd centuries AD. A fortified farmstead on Roman lines is suggested, and with the fort at Carmarthen only a short distance away it is possible; certainly the site would have had a strategic value, with views south and across Carmarthen Bay.

3. Amroth church is dedicated to St Elidir, a saint whose identity remains uncertain. He may have been St Teilo, who was also known as Eliud, and who was a contemporary of St David. The 4th and 5th century original daub and wattle structure made way in 850 for a more solid small stone church. It is known that in 1150 the church, with 50 acres of sanctuary land, was granted to the Knights Hospitallers, whose Welsh headquarters was at nearby Slebech on the eastern Cleddau. The church was rebuilt on a larger scale circa 1490 by John Elliot, the then owner of Amroth Castle, with the addition of a tower and chapel. However parts of the present nave and chancel can still be traced back to circa 1200. The Calvary Cross, on it's 3 stone steps, is much earlier and dates from circa 900. The school, across the road, survived for just over a hundred years. Built in the 1870s, it closed in 1982, and is now a private residence.

4. Colby Lodge and estate take their name from the industrialist

John Colby who mined in the valley in the early and mid 19th century for anthractie and iron ore. Some of the old workings can still be traced in the grounds. The lodge itself he built in 1803 to a design by the architect John Nash. The woodland gardens were laid out by Samuel Kay, who bought the estate in the late 19th century. A good number of the original rhododendrons planted then, many brought back from the Himalayas by his brother, have survived the years to grace the woodland slopes. The gardens, though not the lodge itself, is now in the hands of the National Trust, and is open during the summer season.

Walk Directions: [-] denotes Point of Interest

1. The walk starts from Amroth sea front [1].

2. Just before the New Inn, assuming you are walking from the Amroth Castle/village end, there is adjacent to the public toilets a track leading inland between 2 houses. The route is marked as a bridleway, with a sign for a horse and rider.

3. Walk between the 2 houses — 1 of which once saw service as a corn mill — and turn immediately right and continue uphill on a wooded track [2]. The tarmac road ahead leads to Amroth Castle Farm only.

4. Continue for nearly a mile/1.5 kilometres to reach a crossroads. Turn left and continue on the public footpath/farm road to Eastlake.

5. Just past the house on the right there is a gap in the fence on the left, just before the farmyard.

6. Go through the gap, cross the track, go through another gap and turn right — public footpath sign here.

7. Continue ahead, keeping the cowshed on the right, to shortly reach a stile giving access to a level grassy and wooded path.

8. Continue on the wooded path to reach a concrete bridge across a small stream. Cross the bridge and almost immediately turn right uphill on a path. Ignore the better defined path leading ahead and slightly left.

9. Go ahead to reach a metal gate giving access to a field. Continue on the path between hedge and bank. After a short distance the path meets another field, turns slightly left, and leads on to meet a minor road.

10. Turn right, uphill, to Amroth church [3]. Continue past 'The Old School' — no longer a school, and turn left onto the minor road to Colby Lodge.

11. The public footpath at Colby Lodge [4] is past the 2 car parks and leads left between a walled garden and the Lodge buildings.

12. Keep ahead on the path to meet the minor road from Amroth church. Turn right and walk down to Amroth village.

13. At the junction with the road along the sea front, by the Amroth Arms, turn left to return to the starting point.

Facilities:

Parking also possible at Colby Lodge, or by Amroth church.

Most facilities available in Amroth — a very popular and busy place in summer. Situated as it is on the Carmarthenshire border means that Amroth is the beginning (or end!) of the long distance Pembrokeshire Coast Path. Colby Lodge gardens open April 1 to the beginning of November, tearoom and gallery — National Trust owned. The lodge itself is a private residence and is not open to the public. Amroth Castle offers holiday flats, chalets and caravans. Amroth is the start (or finish) of the Knights' Way, a 9 mile/14.5 kilometre link path between the Coast Path and Blackpool Mill on the eastern Cleddau. Dylan Thomas' Laugharne, and the Boathouse where he wrote, are a few miles up the road in Carmarthenshire.

Other Information

Youth Hostels

There are currently 11 youth hostels in Pembrokeshire. Advance booking may be required during peak holiday season. Location and phone numbers as below:

Broad Haven: *Broad Haven, Haverfordwest SA62 3JH. Tel: 01437 781688.*

Lawrenny: *Millenium Youth Hostel, Lawrenny, Kilgetty SA68 0PN. Tel: 01646 651270.*

Manorbier: *Manorbier, Nr Tenby SA70 7TT. Tel: 01834 871803.*

Marloes Sands: *Runwayskiln, Marloes, Haverfordwest SA62 3BH. Tel: 01646 636667.*

Newport: *Lower St Mary's Street, Newport SA42 0TS. Tel: 01239 820080.*

Pentlepoir (Saundersfoot): *The Old School, Pentlepoir, Saundersfoot SA9 9BJ. Tel: 01834 812333.*

Penycwm (Solva): *Hafod Lodge, Whitehouse, Penycwm, Nr Solva SA62 6LA. Tel: 01437 720959.*

Poppit Sands: *Sea View, Poppit, St Dogmaels, Cardigan SA43 3LP. Tel: 01239 612936.*

Pwll Deri: *Castell Mawr, Trefasser, Goodwick SA64 0LR. Tel: 01348 891233.*

St David's: *Llaethdy, St David's SA62 6PR. Tel: 01437 720345.*

Trevine (Trefine): *11 Ffordd yr Afon, Trefin SA62 5AU. Tel: 01348 831414.*

WALKS IN SNOWDONIA

Walks in North Snowdonia

REVISED EDITION   DON HINSON

WALKS IN SNOWDONIA

New Walks in Snowdonia

REVISED EDITION   DON HINSON

PEMBROKESHIRE WALKS

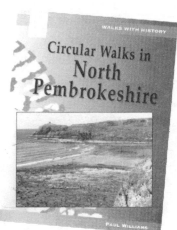

LLŶN PENINSULA WALKS

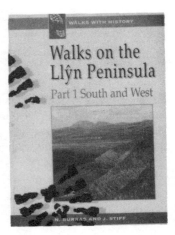